DATE DUE			

WESTERN INTERESTS
IN THE PACIFIC REALM

Studies in Political Science

WESTERN INTERESTS in the PACIFIC REALM

• • •

THOMAS R. ADAM
New York University

RANDOM HOUSE · NEW YORK

FIRST PRINTING

© Copyright, 1967, by Random House, Inc.
All rights reserved under International and Pan-American
Copyright Conventions. Published in New York by Random
House, Inc., and simultaneously in Toronto, Canada, by Random House
of Canada Limited.
Library of Congress Catalog Card Number: 67-22332
Manufactured in the United States of America
by The Colonial Press, Inc., Clinton, Mass.
Typography by Leon Bolognese

Contents

WESTERN INTERESTS
IN THE PACIFIC REALM

INTRODUCTION •
A NOTE ON
THE PACIFIC REALM

If we draw a bold line on a map to link diverse cultural and political systems within vast areas of land and sea, we merely satisfy a creative urge. If we form an arbitrary realm—even in the guise of a paper cut-out—we are simply imposing a personal order on the complexity of stubborn human divisions and interests. Nevertheless, it has become a necessary prelude to the study of international affairs to divide the world into identifiable regions. It amounts, however, to little more than a technique of study and a form of shorthand for simple communication. The realities of social union are too complex to be resolved into easy terms of geographic continuity, climatic similarities, or even ethnic and cultural origins. Regions emerge in clear outline or waver indeterminately over the face of the map in closer accordance with the intent of their originators

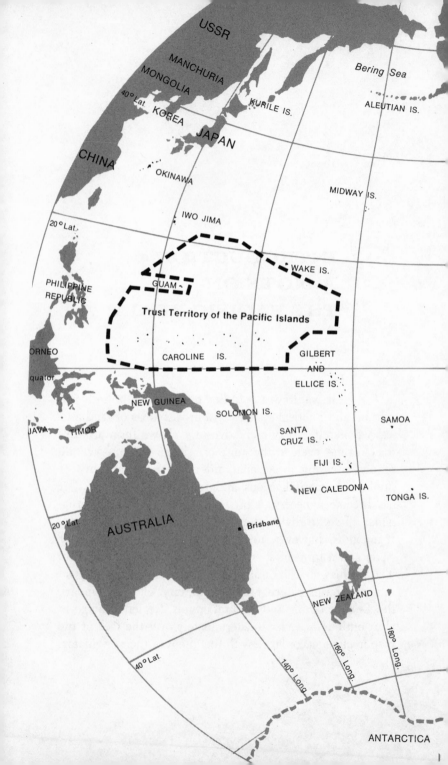

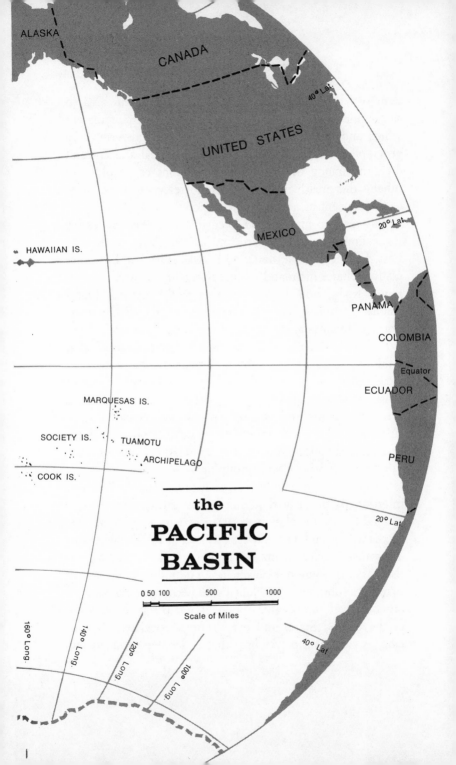

the

PACIFIC
BASIN

0 50 100   500   1000

Scale of Miles

than through their underlying identity. Thus an area in southern and eastern Asia that is associated with circulatory winds and heavy seasonal rainfalls is aptly described by geographers as "monsoon Asia." The political and cultural divisions among the hundreds of millions of people who inhabit this area may be considered irrelevant to the value of the concept of a geographic region.[1]

The terms commonly accepted in the United States for the delimitation of southern and eastern Asia are the Far East, Southeast Asia, and South Asia. The Far East generally includes mainland China, Mongolia, Taiwan, Korea, Hong Kong, and Japan, together with adjacent island chains. Southeast Asia is composed of the Philippines, Borneo, Indonesia, Malaysia, Cambodia, Thailand, Vietnam, Laos, and perhaps Burma. South Asia embraces India, Pakistan, Afghanistan, and the Indian border states—an area formerly designated "the Indian subcontinent." Though satisfactory for many purposes, these sweeping divisions leave gaps in the understanding of political, economic, and cultural relations between the peoples thus arbitrarily classified and complicate the nature of relations between the Western and Asian-Pacific groupings.

Because the purpose of this study is to examine Western interests, particularly though not exclusively those of the United States, in relation to Asian peoples in general, emphasis will be laid on the territorial area of the Pacific basin. This area is selected on the grounds of political pragmatism: this is where our power lies. The military superiority that gives substance to diplomatic and economic claims rests on control of the oceanic sphere. From the point of view of the United States and her Western associates, the Pacific, as such, is a power base that is decisive as far as our interests in Asia and Australasia are concerned. The North Pacific also constitutes a vital defense barrier for the western shores of the United States. The island chain from the Aleutians through Japan, Taiwan, the Philippines, and Borneo to the Malay peninsula serves as a gateway through which the West may still make its influence felt on the affairs of the Asian mainland. From Hawaii to the Moluccas, the Central Pacific is a bastion of the West. Indonesia alone intrudes from the Indian Ocean to provide competition to our hegemony of the South Pacific region.

No geographic justification can be ventured for treating this area as a single region, nor are there ethnic, economic, or political similarities of sufficient weight to be reasonably identified. The earlier diplomatic concept of an area of influence and power is the frankest excuse for bundling such diversities into a single package for the purposes of policy. Demarcation of a "Pacific realm" as a basis for study of Western-Asian relations presents several advantages.[2] "Realm," as opposed to "region," is a political concept bearing the connotation of a domain that is founded on power and control. Though a historical taint of colonialism clings to the fact of dominion, it does not necessarily vitiate it: dominion existed before it assumed the specific guise of colonial rule and is likely to continue after that particular form of control is forsworn. In practice, it signifies the existence of superior power that is exercised in favor of the will and interests of the power holder but not inevitably against either the consent or advantage of the less powerful.

The Pacific realm discussed in this study is centered in the island bases of Western power and radiates with varying strength into the insular and peninsular nations that provide access to the mainland of Asia. Thailand and the former French possessions of Indochina may be regarded as a shadowy borderland between the Pacific realm and the Asian mainland. Should the United States and the West fail to initiate a reasonable policy for the Pacific realm under their direct and indirect guidance, increasing numbers of the constituent peoples may be expected to exercise such a choice for themselves, and not necessarily in our favor.

1 • THE WEST AND
THE PACIFIC REALM

Conquest, conversion, and trade provided the tripodal base from which our Western culture erupted into Asia through the Pacific and Indian oceans. Conquest and conversion were often undertaken by venturesome individuals who were frustrated by the limitations of their place and era. Trade, on the other hand, served the structural pattern of an evolving technology. Through instrumentalities of military domination, organizing skills, and specific cultural values, trade was established and maintained on terms that Western peoples have believed (and with considerable reason) to be favorable to their own prosperity. Western civilization bartered its technology in the form of tools, skills, and investment capital in return for resources, which were won from the soil almost wholly by manual labor. It may be noted that in the bargaining process, its superiority of weapons was a major selling point for Western technology. It is reasonable to claim, however, that the total results of European intervention in the affairs of Asia have proved beneficial, at least to the extent that the inhabitants have been readied for the introduction of technological culture.

Asia and the Pacific region are now undergoing a transition from colonialism to an equal association of free peoples. That is the specific situation confronting the United States. During the colonial period, the European powers held the primary responsibility in this area, but the United States has become the inheritor of the checkered residue. This is partly because the military power that underlay Europe's dominance is now under American control; but a more important reason is that the United States has been forced to become the guardian of Western interests. Because it was impracticable to unravel the complex patterns woven from the threads of three hundred years of European enterprise and dominion, the United States has had to take over a going concern, adapting its historic consequences to the exigencies of our world policies. Thus we face the problem of reconciling the emergent nationalism of Asia with the claims of the former European colonial powers and with our own security and economic concerns.

An ideal solution to the American dilemma might be envisaged that could serve as a criterion for the framing of practical policies. In the first place, Western policy would have to be unified, with the United States accorded a predominant voice in recognition of its position as the responsible military protagonist of all Western interests in the area. European powers' historic and diplomatic claims of sovereign national rights in the Eastern hemisphere have become unrealistic. Such claims originated, by and large, from the exercise of force against either indigenous peoples or European rivals already in possession; with the loss of the power to sustain these claims, the rationale of dominion disappears. In the second place, the free peoples of Asia and the Pacific should choose, of their own free will, to associate with the Western complex, in terms of both its basic economic organization and its social standards. This would be desirable, however, only if the West, and the United States in particular, accept merely a minimum responsibility for the support of the national economies or political systems of individual Asian or Pacific communities. Finally, and perhaps most difficult of all to envisage, Communist China and Soviet Russia would have to be effectively estopped from intruding their military or ideological power into the affairs of the new nations of Asia and the Pacific. Sanctions against the recurrence of any form of imperialism in the Eastern hemisphere would have to be sufficiently effective to destroy the hope of communist expansion. These gilded hopes are put forward principally to assess the negative limits of Western policy—that is, so that we can determine what we can afford to surrender or where compromises are possible if the price of realizing our full objectives be deemed too high to pay.

The Pacific area may be considered particularly affected by questions of space and location; neither a convenient land mass nor rimland regions lie under the uncontested authority of Western culture, with the somewhat remote exceptions of Australia and New Zealand. Western mobility of power by sea and air fails to compensate for a lack of territorial bases. It is hardly an exaggeration to declare that the primary, or at least immediate, concern of the

United States as representative of the West in the Orient is the location of a feasible base from which to make its power effective. If full United States sovereignty could be established in such a base and our cultural patterns assimilated there, we would have ideal conditions for extending power over adjoining regions. The geography of the Pacific realm, however, is hardly favorable to United States aspirations in this respect; though American footholds predominate in the watery expanses of the north Pacific Ocean, their value is gravely diminished by factors of space and distance. An apt description, "Pacific island bastions of the United States," has been accorded the island chain that sweeps from the Aleutians through Hawaii to Guam and borders the Asian land mass.[1] Our sovereignty in these lands rests on a true cultural acceptance that guarantees that the sole threat to United States possession would be the military power of an external invader. However, from the viewpoint of an American "presence" in the Pacific realm backed by stable, continuous military power, these holdings appear insufficient in the light of the confusing changes in sea, land, and air forces that are resulting from a fluid weapon technology. Certainly since the Japanese war political and military leaders have remained firm in their conviction that it is imperative for our national security that we acquire additional holdings in the strategic trust territories of the Mariana and Caroline groupings and that we occupy the Japanese-owned Bonin and Ryuku chain.

In the south Pacific Ocean, a negligible, and probably temporary, holding in eastern Samoa represents the extent of direct American sovereignty. Of course, from the political and military point of view, the gap has been filled through a network of treaty arrangements that provide rights to military bases in Australia and the Philippine Republic in return for United States obligations to afford protection. Such arrangements should not be equated, however, with the establishment of a stable power base; by their nature they lie at the mercy of changing political currents over which the United States possesses very limited control. A constant need to bargain, compromise, and delegate authority hinders the formation of consistent policies. The accidents of rising and dying empires have spread a tangled web of extraneous national sovereignties over the island groups of the region and their essential communication systems.

A distinction may be drawn between the establishment of a firm and settled power base and immediate arrangements, necessarily of a transient nature, entered into under the exigencies of a current situation. United States policy in the Pacific at the present time is, perhaps unavoidably, upheld by a patchwork of treaty relations created in the face of transitory power groupings and based on illogical cultural and political foundations. An outstanding example is our obligations toward the Nationalist China regime in Taiwan, which separates us from our Western partners in the region. The development of American-Japanese relations, though generally satisfactory, is again divorced from any joint policy to which our allies can be considered fully committed.

In 1954, when the United States devised its most ambitious attempt at a regional security pact for Southeast Asia, the Southeast Asia Treaty Organization (SEATO), the alliance included only three Asian nations, the Philippine Republic, Thailand, and Pakistan. Though useful as an immediate check against Communist aggression, SEATO is heavily weighted in favor of Western power and influence and lacks the integrating force of common cultural or political interests. Even in the field of common defense, individual commitments stretch no further than a recognition that aggression in the treaty area constitutes a danger to the member nations' own security, obligating action "in accordance with its (national) constitutional processes." It remains highly questionable whether Pakistan or even the Philippines could be relied upon to contribute to military action considered essential by their Western partners.

Crisis diplomacy has clearly ruled American leadership in the Pacific realm, leaving a legacy of abortive projects and inadequately based alliances. The power gap caused by European withdrawal has opened the way to an expansion of Chinese influence, under cover of an aggressive communist ideology. This evokes memories of China's historic cultural imperialism, whose continuity and solidarity have periodically threatened to dominate the area from China's central land mass with its overwhelming population. The cultural survival of the non-Chinese peoples of Asia beyond the Indian subcontinent clearly demands a far-sighted policy of political cooperation, if not outright integration. A pattern has now begun to emerge, however, along probable lines of a limited community that could serve as a focus for Western power. Regional groupings have begun to crystallize around cultural similarities that have been only temporarily masked by the emergent nationalism that replaced European colonialism. Tentative steps toward closer union of peoples of predominantly Malaysian cultural affiliation have led to proposals for a regional organization, at one time named Maphilindo, to unite the nation states of Indonesia, the Philippine Republic, and Malaysia.[2]

There are several possibilities, some mutually exclusive, for the future development of regional groupings in the Pacific realm. On the lowest and least satisfactory level, at least from the point of view of Western interests, policies of national expansion may foster power grabs of adjacent territories, bringing the non-Chinese nations of the Pacific into conflict with one another and rendering all equally vulnerable to the communist giant on the mainland. This possibility was foreshadowed by the tensions surrounding the political union of Malaya, Singapore, Sabah, and Sarawak into the greater state of Malaysia; Indonesia and the Philippines reacted with counterclaims for territorial expansion, endangering the peace of the area. The avoidance of suicidal rivalry between Pacific peoples of similar cultures appears essential for the protection of the Western position. A more attractive possibility lies in the formation of a confederation or even a federation by the insular and peninsular peoples on the borderlands of Asia; a grouping of this nature could, by reason of its cultural integrity and combined military and economic strength, impose limits on any expansionist policies ventured by the mainland colossi, Communist China and Soviet Russia. For Western nations this borderland aggregation might provide an acceptable bridge between their own technological cultures based on free enterprise and the agrarian communities of the Orient. Besides, it should facilitate a welcome shift in the primary responsibility for defense against communist aggression throughout the region without removing the need for Western partnership in the containment of Sino-Soviet power. Encouragement of this form of regional organization will require that active and fully integrated policies be adopted by the United States and its noncommunist associates.

A major obstacle in the way of cooperation between insular and peninsular borderlands of Asia is the equivocal position of the remaining colonial territories in the Pacific, which form what might be described as a communications network of islands serving Western interests. The Melanesian, Micronesian, Polynesian, Papuan, and Negrito peoples may be regarded as culturally neutral and accordingly subject to assimilation into more fully organized communities; this offers a serious temptation to any expansionist rivalry of the Maphilindo nations, should they become convinced that the Western powers do not intend to maintain their former association with these emerging peoples. In short, we must use the remnants of Western colonialism to form a favorable, permanent relationship if a power gap that could lead to internal conflict in the area is to be avoided. For the moment, the West possesses an inestimable advantage in the goodwill of these peoples, who remain, at least temporarily, unstirred by nationalist emotions or ethnic hatreds. Should this boon of fellowship be dissipated through neglect, cultural arrogance, or careless failure to establish common Western policies of association, the abdication of the West in this region will undermine its military capacities and political influence throughout all Asia. On the other hand, if the West proves capable of organizing these territories under its own direct control along lines acceptable to the inhabitants, a true basis will be established for bargaining on equal terms as a responsible participant in Pacific affairs. This kind of partnership in the protection and advancement of an oceanic cultural complex could then serve as a model for the larger task of establishing a mutually advantageous association with the nationalist groups on the insular and peninsular borderlands of Asia.

A further factor inhibiting closer association between the Maphilindo nations is an element of uncertainty concerning the roles that Japan and Australia may play in future Pacific policies. Here again, responsibility rests on the shoulders of Western states, who have let amiable confusion obscure the joint policy within their power to formulate and implement. Suspicions, however unfounded, that the United States and Britain may lend their power to further Australian ambitions in the Pacific area are unavoidable among Asian peoples emerging from centuries of European dominance. The part that Australia will be permitted to play as a representative of Western culture in the region must be clearly defined and delimited if the confidence of the Maphilindo nations is to be won.

Perhaps the trickiest of all the obstacles separating the West from a potential regional organization focused around the Maphilindo nations is the question of direct intervention in Korea, Vietnam, Laos, and Cambodia; in the face of brazen communist aggression, it is not the fact of intervention as such that constitutes the issue but rather its unilateral character, supported as it is by the overwhelming military power of the United States. No equality of association may be anticipated until the major border countries are accorded a voice in policies determining intervention. But perhaps these interventionist episodes are transitory manifestations of an undeclared and inconclusive war between Communist China and the United States. Eventual stalemate might make it desirable in the interests of the United States itself to construct some analogy to the Organization of American States, say an "Organization of Insular and Peninsular Pacific States," to supervise on common terms the conditions of intervention.

Even if all the foregoing factors affecting association between the West and the insular and peninsular nations of the Pacific and Indian oceans were resolved in our favor, the result would not meet the need for a dependable base for the exercise of Western influence and power. Our Asian allies would remain associates bound to us principally by a confluence of interests; attempts to use them to promote specific concerns of the United States and her European partners would almost certainly destroy the structure of association. For the forseeable future, then, some physical center of Western interests must be constituted from territories over which Western nations possess direct sovereignty. Organization of such a center along regional lines presents problems of considerable political as well as economic complexity; probably it would not be worth the trouble and expense involved if there were reasonable alternatives for the preservation of Western interests in the Pacific realm. It is only by facing the distasteful prospect of a fortress America linked to a fortress Europe that any true perspective of possible Pacific policies may be gained. If, at the close of the colonial epoch, we hope to maintain some reasonable fragment of the historic connection between the two portions of the world, something more substantial than floating or airborne power must mark our presence. Gun-boat commerce (even if armed with hydrogen bombs) is no longer practicable, and without commerce our cultural ties with the Orient wither into nothingness. Only the doughtiest believers in the efficacy of economic competition to overcome all obstacles and unite all peoples would remain confident that we could maintain our links with Asia without participating directly in its affairs through the exercise of power and influence. It appears wiser to accept the fact that we are engaged in a serious struggle for cultural survival that involves the continuous presence of Western-oriented communities as participating members among the peoples of Pacific and Asian lands.

Commerce, not conquest, forms the positive motivation impelling our technological culture to concern itself in the economic, social, and political organization of the agrarian masses of Asia. It is difficult, however, to apply meaningful quantitative standards to Western economic interests in Asia and the Pacific. A tempting but misleading generalization would be the assertion that while Asia is desperately dependent for its future progress on our well-developed industrial complex, we, on the other hand, would suffer little more than a minor setback to our economic advancement should Asia cease to exist as a source of raw materials or as a market for our products. The missing factor in this soothing proposition lies in the assumption that, if we disowned Asia, her struggling millions would remain, as in the past, wholly absorbed in food production on a survival level and consequently incapable of intervening in our affairs. It is not always easy to view our own Western culture in its proper historical perspective as a minority movement of recent date in the evolution of civilization, as one among several possible formulas for the organization of society, one that has been accepted by the bulk of mankind principally on the pragmatic record of its operation over the course of a few centuries. But, should our Western solution prove inapplicable in practice to the bread-and-butter problems of a majority of living people, no inherent reasons support its continued monopoly of the design of social development.

In crude political terms, if Western technology fails to spread its benefits to the majority of the world's peoples in underdeveloped areas, may they not resort to age-old violences of war and rebellion to counter our economic superiority and raise their own alternative cultural experiments on the resulting ruins? This, of course, is the thesis adopted by Mao Tse-tung to rally the discontented among the peoples of the underdeveloped regions to the banner of Chinese communism. To the United States, and to the West in general, it presents a challenge to show in practice the universal, or more mildly world, value of our industrial enterprise system; if we fail, we must defend our privileges and gains by means of the continuing, brutalizing, and costly exercise of superior force in every corner of the globe.

Though the Western literary imagination has long been fascinated by the "riches of the Orient," they have largely escaped statistical scrutiny, particularly in terms of their effects on Western economies. Unquestionably, individuals and social oligarchies have profited handsomely from the European intrusion into Asia; the English "nabobs" of the eighteenth century, for example, almost wrecked the ruling structure of British society with the corruptive insolence of their booty. When the total domestic economy of an imperial Western nation is taken into account, however, results appear less sensational. Thus Britain at the apogee of her empire in 1936 counted her trade with Southeast Asia, excluding Burma, at less than 2 percent of her total foreign trade.[3] British exports to China, Japan, Malaya, the Dutch East Indies, and Thailand during the same period merely equaled her exports to Canada. Qualitative factors relating to the infrastructure of world shipping and competitive advantages in access to certain raw materials, particularly rubber and tin, introduced additional beneficial factors. By and large, however, the political empires of Europe in the East were of transitory economic value to their originators, for they failed to establish a symbiotic relationship between the Western and Eastern economies.

Since the collapse of empire, the flow of trade between Europe and Asia has deteriorated, at least as far as the interests of Asia's peoples are concerned. This has been due perhaps to shifts in Western industrial and financial structures that appear unlikely to be reversed. Yet underdeveloped countries are largely dependent on their export products for the technological capital required to promote internal development. Though industrial expansion in the West might be expected to increase demand for raw materials, this is true only under conditions where technology remains static. During the last three decades, technical discoveries have in practice enabled industrial production in the United States to be increased twice as fast as the consumption of raw materials.

The 1962 Report of the United Nations Economic Commission for Asia and the Far East (ECAFE) offers some sober conclusions concerning the present direction of East-West trade:

> While export trade is of critical importance to the economic development of less developed countries its recent performance in the developing ECAFE region has been disquieting. Growth of exports of the region has lagged not only behind that of developed areas and other less developed areas, but even behind the growth of the aggregate product of the region. Its capacity of raising income and employment and of obtaining capital goods

from abroad is therefore being weakened. . . . The export lag is deeply rooted in the structure of exports and production patterns of these countries. The region relies heavily on primary exports, particularly of raw materials, to the developed areas among which western Europe is the most important. Primary exports have been for a long time showing a stagnant if not declining trend, with wide fluctuations. In contrast to the rapid expansion of world trade, their recent performance has been especially disappointing. Raw material exports from the developing ECAFE region have risen much more slowly and those to the EEC area have actually declined. Apparently even a high rate of growth in the developed countries may not guarantee a high rate of exports from the region, unless the region is enabled to export a large amount of those commodities for which the demand is sensitive to growth. As though this situation is not gloomy enough, the region's exports are encountering some uncertainty or even adverse effects from the establishment of the European Common Market.[4]

Table 1, compiled by the Economic Commission for Asia and the Far East, illustrates the relatively minor position occupied by the countries of Asia in the overall perspective of international trade.

Of course, qualitative factors concerning types of product exported might weigh heavily in any estimate of the dependence of Western industrialism on the contributions of Asia. But the list of principal exports from the region set out in Table 2 fails to indicate any irreplaceable source of raw materials essential to the functioning of Western economies. Tropical Africa and Latin America are capable of bulk production of practically all the materials involved, with the possible exceptions of copra and jute.

TABLE 1 · Total Value of Exports and Imports of
the Developing ECAFE Region[a] as Compared with
the World Totals   (*In Millions of Dollars*)

	1928	1938	1948	1959–1961 Average
Exports (FOB)				
A. World	$55,222	$23,500	$57,300	$125,213
B. Developing ECAFE Region	5,595	2,256	4,694	7,482
Percentage of B in A	10.1%	9.6%	8.2%	6.0%
Imports (CIF)				
C. World	$60,080	$25,400	$63,500	$129,213
D. Developing ECAFE Region	4,597	1,829	5,089	8,804
Percentage of D in C	7.6%	7.2%	8.0%	6.8%

[a] Excluding Japan and mainland China.
SOURCE: *Economic Survey of Asia and the Far East, 1962* (New York:
United Nations, 1963), p. 7.

A further long-term factor mitigating against Asian
trade with advanced technological cultures is suggested in
the *1964 Economic Survey of Asia and the Far East:*

> The deterioration, however, in the terms of trade goes
> far beyond foodstuffs. Highly subsidized exports of cot-
> ton from the United States have reduced the potential
> export earnings of some Asian producers, as have re-
> strictions, imposed to help domestic interests, on its im-
> ports of lead, zinc and petroleum. But the greatest danger
> to exports of materials has come from technical progress
> in making synthetic substitutes for such major Asian
> exports as rubber and jute, or in economizing inputs of
> materials and metals in manufacturing processes. This

TABLE 2 · Developing ECAFE Region[a]: Distribution of Exports of Principal Commodities by Destination (1958–1960 average)

	Total value of exports (in millions of dollars)	Percent distribution						
		OUTSIDE REGIONS[b]	UK	EEC	WESTERN EUROPE	EASTERN EUROPE	NORTH AMERICA	JAPAN
Rubber	$1,157.8	98.0%	18.3%	20.4%	42.7%	13.0%	25.0%	9.1%
Tea	534.2	95.7	50.9	4.0	58.3	3.6	11.0	0.4
Crude petroleum	440.8	89.5	19.7	18.3	42.9	0.05	13.7	9.5
Petroleum products	409.2	46.6	6.8	4.4	13.7	0.01	0.6	2.4
Rice	345.1	33.0	1.2	4.4	5.9	2.8	—	9.1
Sugar	195.7	80.2	—	—	—	—	57.3	18.0
Copra	175.4	94.0	3.3	40.8	50.9	—	29.7	5.1
Cotton fabrics	174.0	79.1	28.7	1.2	30.6	0.1	9.1	—
Jute	166.5	92.0	23.3	34.6	64.5	7.1	7.8	5.0
Jute fabrics	154.5	96.8	8.7	2.4	14.0	1.9	58.1	0.1
Tin metal	119.9	91.4	3.7	15.1	20.4	0.3	45.4	16.0
Cotton, raw	91.2	76.7	9.8	16.5	26.7	11.7	1.9	43.1
Tobacco	66.1	94.8	35.0	40.4	82.4	2.1	6.2	0.1
Tin-in-concentrate	63.0	60.5	22.9	4.0	27.0	—	30.9	0.2
Coconut oil	51.6	83.6	2.6	25.8	28.6	3.4	42.8	—
Palm oil	39.1	79.0	19.9	38.5	58.5	0.1	7.3	6.5
TOTAL	$4,184.1	82.9%	18.4%	14.2%	35.8%	5.0%	19.1%	7.3%

[a] Including Iran.
[b] Including Japan.

SOURCE: *Economic Survey of Asia and the Far East, 1962* (New York: United Nations, 1963), p. 22.

competition, of course, is on a different footing from the various types of protection, although synthetics have sometimes been subsidized in one way or another; it is reasonable to demand the removal of barriers to trade, but hardly reasonable to demand a halting of technical progress.[5]

Though vested interests of long-established international trading corporations, generally of British or European origin, remain a core of economic involvement, involving many millions of dollars in a cash nexus, they have become during the past decade more of a holding operation than a dynamic incentive to link the economies of Western and Eastern communities. That flexible tool of Western industrial expansion, private investment capital, has found the Asian climate unattractive in comparison with other areas competing for its attention. According to the Economic Commission for Asia and the Far East, "over 90 percent of the capital received by ECAFE countries during 1951–1960 was on official account and the inflow of private capital was negligible." [6] Lacking motivation from the private sector of Western national economies, relations between Asia and the West have centered, perhaps unduly, on governmental policies. Though cultural contacts remain vigorous, a decline in missionary undertakings has removed a popular base for such contacts; now the approach is more intellectual and scholarly and appeals to narrower segments of both communities.

By and large, the pattern to be followed in future dealings between Asian and Western nation-states rests in the hands of political leaders and their technical advisors, a responsibility that is insecurely rooted in the understanding or concern of the peoples themselves. Accordingly, a capacity to visualize future needs while relating them to the current interests of the community will be the principal instrument for establishing lasting harmony between the two hemispheres.

Statesmanship operates most effectively from a power base, and the United States is now the repository of the major portion of Western military strength in the Pacific region. Perhaps the transition from the empires of Europe and Japan came about too suddenly for the American community to appraise its new responsibility properly. Certainly it occurred as a military event, with the consequence that its military aspects have dominated official and public attention. But military strength has meaning only in terms of political and economic purposes, and American long-term objectives in the Pacific region have not yet been clearly defined. Of course, the fundamental issue of the defense of the nation's shores from attack by sea or air provides solid grounds for mastery of the Pacific Ocean, or at least for ensuring that it remains in friendly hands. As a principal base for present policies, however, it is questionable whether this explanation would prove acceptable even to our military command.

One obvious justification for United States intervention in Asian affairs lies in our leadership of the world struggle against communism. Communist political and economic infiltration among a majority of the world's peoples appears to American political leadership to be fatal to our safety and progress; this attitude is supported almost unanimously by public opinion. In consequence, we have tended to fight the spread of communism wherever it appears likely to break through its established boundaries, without taking into full account the fact that we would be subsequently involved in the protection and guarantee of alien economies and political systems. The policy of military intervention, forsworn in Latin America (at least for the time being), has been transferred to Southeast Asia as an instrument of United States statesmanship. It may not, however, be called a joint policy of the Occidental nations, for American leadership in this field has outrun the enthusiasm of our European associates. Notwithstanding, it is our policy, and it is accepted by the bulk of the electorate as inevitable until some workable alternative can be suggested.

An exclusively military emphasis may have the effect of weakening rather than strengthening the impact of this policy. Though under favorable circumstances a communist system may be imposed on a people against their consent through military conquest, it is not equally true that the containment of communism may be guaranteed by military encirclement. The global Cold War is being transformed into a struggle between economic and social systems that are competing for the allegiance of political communities at diverse levels of technological advancement. It is the operative systems, working on the level of material production, cultural standards, and fair distribution, that are being weighed in the balance by the yet uncommitted peoples. Committed nations on a high level of technology, whether capitalist or communist, appear in slight danger of being overwhelmed by each other's propaganda. Only unbalanced fanatics would consider the total destructiveness of war essential to settle the present argument between rival technologies on their home grounds.

The unknown factor, the one that is disruptive to the continuing patterns of our free society, is to be found in the attitude of the majority of world peoples who have not reached the level of technological progress achieved by either Western nations or Soviet Russia. The assumption that underdeveloped communities will remain content to forswear technology is untenable; a belief that they have no alternative but to follow our lead is demonstrably false; a smug certainty that communism must inevitably lead to a worsening rather than betterment of existing miseries constitutes a foolish illusion. It is wiser to face the fact that we are fairly matched in a historic struggle of competing systems, to realize that our survival depends on our own continuing efforts and wisdom and not on the inevitable justice of history.

2 • THE CONSEQUENCES
OF WESTERN DOMINION

A reassessment of the colonial period in the Pacific and Indian oceans, particularly of its final stages, appears relevant to a formulation of realistic policies. Colonialism is a generic term, however, that covers a series of relationships that spread over a considerable interval of historic time and changed radically in character. The culminating relation between ruler and ruled in European colonial territories provides the most obvious guide to present patterns of contact. Between the earlier and later epochs of colonial domination, a fundamental shift occurred from power-based rule to approximations of consensual government that foreshadowed the rise of national unity. In the birth throes of these nations, passive acceptance of the institutional authority provided by European administrators was a temporary shelter against communal rivalries.

When the twentieth-century spirit of nationalism, spreading with almost religious force, subordinated communalism and tribalism throughout the region, the artificial cement of European domination became superfluous.

Nevertheless, the particular manifestations of nationalism were directly affected by the pattern of the institutional culture under which they were nurtured. For example, independent India and Pakistan still retain institutional and cultural traces of their origin in British India; present distinctions between the Philippine Republic, Malaysia, and Indonesia may be interpreted as the result of Spanish, American, British, and Dutch administrative and cultural practices. Though influence has replaced power as the bond between Western and Asian peoples, the link has not weakened into historic sentimentality.

At the present time, technology is playing a greater part than ideology in the spread of common institutional patterns among the world's peoples. Even in the political sphere, popular government has largely replaced dynastic or oligarchic rule more as a consequence of technical advances in communication than through revolutionary changes in outlook.

For practical purposes of policy making in the field of Asian-Western relations, ideological and emotional differences are less important than the development of those economic and political patterns that are shown by pragmatic experiment to be essential to the development of technology. A foundation for such patterns was laid down under colonial conditions throughout the greater part of Asia. Because Europe and North America were engaged principally in promoting their own industrial techniques, the organization of Asian peoples under their domination reflected this paramount interest. Asian critics are perhaps correct in claiming that the indigenous economy was arbitrarily subordinated to provide advantages for more advanced industrial centers overseas; that future integration of agrarian communities into technological culture was ill-planned or even disregarded in favor of securing immediate profits to Western entrepreneurs. Nevertheless, the penetration of Asian societies with the seed of technology was accomplished, however roughly, establishing thereby an irreversible connection between cultural systems in the major regions of the world.

Colonial rule, then, should be reevaluated in terms of the particular institutional pattern created as a matrix for the character of the emergent national states. It may be ventured that political forms, particularly those based on Western ideologies, proved the least successful of the institutional exchanges. Representative government certainly was initiated, though not wholly implemented, throughout major regions of the Asian and Pacific area. It is arguable, however, that advances in physical communication made consultation with the general and local communities essential to the operation of a governmental system commanding precariously slight instruments of force. Under colonial conditions, the availability of troops and governing personnel was strictly limited by factors of expense and manpower. Accordingly, a rapid growth in communication systems that spread information and supplied the capacity for mass organization forced the development of consensual institutions. In varying degrees, the British, Dutch, American, and French regimes in Asia and the Pacific introduced what they claimed to be representative democracy, though their programs appeared more immediately concerned with

the administrative exigencies resulting from the social up-
heavals brought about by technological change.

On both political and administrative levels, more divergencies than similarities marked the colonial regimes of the
Western nations. Britain and the United States, for example, displayed a racial hubris absent, in general, from
their equally self-seeking rivals in the race for empire. Consequently, the colonial connection in areas under the rule
of France or Portugal had different social implications than
would be found among peoples subjected to Anglo-Saxon
condescensions.

An understandable eagerness to wipe the slate clean of
the colonial process tends to blind the American viewpoint
to realities of the current situation. It was hoped that a
more or less united Western complex of technologically
and industrially advanced nations could make a new start
there, cooperating for mutual advantage with an independent Asia emerging from an agrarian economy. In the first
place, however, a united Western society of nations has yet
to prove itself to Asian eyes; in terms of historic experience,
Asian and Pacific peoples have endured the role of pawns
in the game of ferocious rivalries that constituted European struggles for empire. Indonesians, who have watched
their leaders playing skillfully on vestiges of these rivalries
to hasten independence and gain further territory, would
be as little likely to dismiss them into the mists of history
as would the Vietnamese, still torn apart by the conflict of
contending saviors. The role of Asia and the Pacific as a
convenient checkerboard for European power politics looms
too recent in memory to be obliterated by the Pax Ameri-
cana enforced by the Seventh Fleet. Apart from all too
recent history, there is little acceptable evidence of common

Western policies for the region as a whole or its constituent parts. United States military superiority and the comparative powerlessness of the former empires does not constitute agreement on far-reaching economic and political relations between the two major regions of the world. Though it is obvious that no Western policy could subsist without United States acceptance and implementation, American might is a substitute for, rather than a fulfillment of, Western policy under existing conditions.

In the second place, political independence did not coincide with a clean break between Asian and Western economies that would permit a fresh start to be made in the untainted air of a brave new world. Technological change and the beginnings of industrialism had roots in the colonial era that created special patterns of trade and economic growth linking particular regions to specific European and North American economies. Indonesia and the Philippines, for example, were far apart at the time of independence because their economic structures had been forcibly linked to the divergent foci of the Netherlands and the United States. Institutional continuity in the economic sphere remains a powerful force attaching specific Asian economies to those of specific Western nations.

British colonial rule in Asian and Pacific lands reflected an intricate pattern of commercial and cultural traits projected overseas by Britain in the arrogance of her power. An image remains, fortunately divested of accidental superiority, that continues to contribute to the larger question of relations between Oriental and Western cultures. Certain elements of the British colonial experience can be a guide to present and future relations between the two cultural regions. Though it would be pleasant to disregard a naked power factor as an outmoded historical anachronism, caution dictates at least a temporary acceptance of this element as a continuing feature of the West's position in the area. Britain, as the most successful protagonist of sea power during the nineteenth century, exploited its control of communications between Europe and Asia as a basis for a commercial and political empire. Alternative land routes under the less enterprising sway of Czarist Russia lagged both quantitatively and technologically. Mastery of sea routes may be accounted merely a preliminary step to the establishment of the imposing façade of political control of the Indian subcontinent, carrying with it some of the shadowy influence historic India exercised over the peninsular and insular borders of Asia. However, it can now be seen that the English were incapable, for reasons internal to their own culture, of any true conquest of the varied peoples of India and its surrounding oceans: the English did not try to bring about full cultural assimilation, even in the role of a governing class, and permanent association between governed and governors was impracticable if this cultural accord was evaded. Hence the British in India and elsewhere were primarily middlemen between their own nascent industrial culture and the countries that might serve as their markets as well as producers of needed raw materials. Colonial government was thus almost incidental to the major objective of a pattern of commerce based on physical control of basic lines of communication.

A switch from British sea power to United States sea and air power has left the outlines of Western superiority in communications largely unchanged. Of course, technological change, particularly in the air and missile field, lessens the capacity of the West to maintain positive use of its lines of communication; on the other hand, the United States and its associates can deny their opponents significant freedom of physical movement throughout the Indian and Pacific oceans. From the nonmilitary point of view, the technical and commercial apparatus of communications, ships, planes, and insurance channels remains firmly in Western hands and constitutes a service mechanism for trade that could not readily be dispensed with by Asian peoples. The existing British-European pattern of communications, though now overlaid by American additions and affected by change in the political situation, is still an indispensable link essential to the prosperity of both cultural systems.

Britain's most lasting impact upon the Far East may stem from the version of laissez-faire economic organization that marked the birth of her own industrial revolution. Her commercial and political supremacy in the Indian and Pacific oceans during the nineteenth century made it easy for her to impose her own domestic pattern on the beginnings of technological change throughout the region without having to pay much regard to whether that pattern was relevant to traditional social structures. Nonetheless, enterprise capital proved a useful incentive to fruitful social change in the subcontinent of India and its environs and inspired that greatest of all Western imitators, the empire of Japan. On the other hand, conspicuous failures for progressive capitalism, exemplified in the mainland of China and Burma, illustrate a historic linkage between acceptance of capitalism and tolerance of British or American administrative and economic patterns.

Commercial and political relations between West and East were maintained over a sufficient length of time to permit these disparate systems to evolve similar institutional responses to matters of common concern. In general, traditional Asian social systems adjusted to the alien factor of technology by passively imitating the industrial ideology of their colonial tutor. The differences among European nations in the pace and direction of the industrial revolution accordingly affected the beginnings of industrial technology throughout Asia by marking them with the stamp of their British, French, Dutch, or American colonial origin. These divergent roots of Asian economies must still be taken into account in assessing patterns of linkage between Western and Asian cultures. British influence where it was successful, as in India, Malaya, Fiji, and Pacific island groupings, most closely approximated present-day American capitalism in its emphasis on private as opposed to state enterprise and a corresponding concept of the free market in domestic and international terms.

Political independence has added a competitive element that had been partly suppressed in relation to the metropolitan economy during the colonial period: the new nations claim equal status within the capitalist sphere. This should, however, enhance the close bonds with corresponding Western systems if sensible policies are adopted recognizing the justice of the change. The long-established networks that link the finance and commerce of specific Asian lands to European and American counterparts should be openly recognized as important to the preservation of basic Western interests. Western commercial rivalries, which have been traditionally associated with power politics, linger on in that portion of the world where communism has achieved a power advantage that can be countered, if at all, only by confrontation with a united and indivisible Western organization.

The organization of administrative government reflected the capacity or incapacity of colonial regimes to identify themselves with indigenous cultural traditions and processes. Because the social detachment of the British from their subject peoples was particularly marked, greater efficiency was required of British rule in terms of an impersonal administrative structure than was true of the regimes imposed by the French, Dutch, or Portuguese. Accordingly, from India through Malaya, the inhabitants developed an attitude toward political government that permitted them to treat it as a service institution; they might judge the effectiveness of that government in terms of their own prosperity and well-being, but they did not admit any responsibility for either practical or moral participation in its operation. This clinical tradition of politics tempered the mood of nations freeing themselves from British dominion, so that nationalist independence expressed itself more in the replacement of alien by indigenous rulers than in any overturn of the system of rule in favor of increased participation by the individual in affairs of state. The substance of independent sovereignty formed comfortably enough around a durable administrative skeleton inherited from the British that allowed for continuity on a pragmatic basis. Malaya, now Malaysia, provides an excellent example of the part played by British colonial techniques in the formation of a modern Asian nation and in the determination of its political character. Bringing together separate sultanates and establishing seeds of national identity in the absence of any popular movement was a delicate and well-executed essay in administrative art that was gravely complicated by the existence of two cultural groups almost equal in numbers, the native Malays and immigrant Chinese. Operating with minimum emotional commitment to either group, the British created an administrative pattern that provided each element of the plural society with at least a tolerable satisfaction of communal needs. To the Malay, the system granted an opportunity to compensate for economic inferiority through preference in government employment. The Chinese community, for its part, was protected from political persecution in its favored pursuits of individual and collective enterprise; this enabled the Chinese to achieve social power through their contributions to the country's economy. Independence has proved that nationalism can flourish in a markedly plural society organized under a federal system if the administrative apparatus has been built firmly enough to take the strain.

Western political ideologies, on the other hand, are of dubious significance in the governmental and social patterns of independent Asia. Their alien origin, unrelated to religious or cultural traditions of Oriental peoples, deprived them of emotional impact; besides, their advocacy by Westerners contradicted the actual practices through which European rulers maintained their colonial dominion. Devices such as representative assemblies did prove acceptable, because they added to a deep-rooted tradition of popular control over rulers a practical means of implementing this control through technical improvements in communication. But deeper philosophies of individual freedom, equality, or the rule of law lacked the background of historic and cultural tradition that marked their emergence in Europe and North America. In practice, Western social theory has influenced Asian communities almost entirely through a native elite subjected to a Western educational process. Power elites educated in London, Paris, or the United States apply distinctive interpretations of Western theory to problems of their respective environments. Though British, French, and American political concepts may in this way influence Asian development, a generalized Western political philosophy has not taken hold either in the understanding of Asian masses or in the intellectual commitments of present rulers. History, language, and educational systems have forged bonds too disparate in nature to be generalized under a single rubric relating the West to the Orient.

Because the British impact in the Pacific and Indian ocean region extended over wide areas that were peopled by inhabitants of diverse cultural standards, its outstanding characteristic was adaptability. Rather than being conquered, the great land mass of India was infiltrated through a technique of participating in the local political turmoil until the English emerged as a governing class still within the historic continuity of Indian tradition. As a nineteenth-century British administrator admitted, "the imperial sign manual had been at the disposal of any adventurer or usurper . . . who could overcome the powerless court and dictate his own investiture with some lofty office. . . ." [1] Two factors in the Indian success story affected British patterns of control throughout its subsequent colonial empire; first, the value of retaining at least the outward forms of indigenous authority patterns, as in the case of the Indian princely states, and second, the imposition of order as a thing in itself that overrode all social and ideological tensions with a neutral Pax Britannica under which commerce could flourish and its fruits compensate for vanished liberties. Continuity of order may become habitual if institutional foundations are realistic, and it is to such underpinnings rather than generalized philosophies that former British territories look for the heritage of their Western connection.

The North American impact on Pacific and Asian affairs has differed in kind as well as degree from that of Europe. Motivated in its origin by the Yankee trading spirit, interest in the Pacific underwent subtle change with the settlement of the West Coast. The phrase "manifest destiny" sponsored a passing wave of imperialist expansion, inaugurated perhaps by Secretary Seward's annexation of the Midway Island group in 1867. Though the tide of popular opinion in favor of an American Pacific empire soon ebbed, the acquisition of Hawaii, the Philippines, and American Samoa committed the United States to the power struggle in the Pacific as a full participant. Hereditary distaste for European colonialism induced the sovereign American people to demand that administration of overseas possessions follow the consensual pattern of the domestic polity. Almost by happenstance, a miracle of cultural integration transformed Hawaii into an exemplary meeting place of Western and Pacific peoples. In the Philippines, some rough and turbulent beginnings progressed to as practical and profitable an exchange of Western technology and Asian cultural values as has occurred anywhere in Asia or the Pacific. Guam, on a lesser scale, has followed the Hawaiian precedent; American Samoa and the trust territories of the Mariannas are being handled with painstaking solicitude. What is lacking is a proper realization of the consequences of empirical American successes in providing working relations with Pacific peoples. The irreversible spread of modern technology ensures continuously increasing contact between Pacific communities and the Western economic and social organization. Political independence to some extent eases the way for freer association; it is, however, no substitute for a mutual responsibility for development. A negative American fear of communist expansion obscures a lack of planning for positive Western association. We have allowed our opponents to steal the initiative and thunder "neocolonialism" at timid efforts to maintain continuity with past successes. If Hawaii and the Philippines can be regarded as flexible solutions to the impact of technology on Pacific peoples, our failure to build on these empirical triumphs is an abnegation of legitimate American influence in this region.

Two major elements must be faced by the American people in meeting responsibilities in the Pacific realm in terms of United States security and workable world relations. In the first place, a decision must be taken about the degree of political association we are prepared to grant to peoples of different cultural background. Though we have accepted the polyglot culture of Hawaii and the Spanish-oriented mores of Puerto Rico, the Philippines were dismissed somewhat summarily from free association with the mainland community of North America. The position of the inhabitants of our strategic trust territories and of Samoa is ambiguous, indicating that we are not yet ready to accord equal status within our domestic community to Pacific peoples who might desire to link themselves with the American system. In this respect we show to poor advantage beside France: all inhabitants of that nation's island territories rank as French citizens. Our attitude imposes a necessity of political independence on island communities topographically and economically ill-suited to bear this burden. Deep-seated racial and cultural prejudice among the older power centers in United States politics renders it unrealistic to expect an acknowledgment of human dignity sufficiently generous to attract the diverse cultures of the Pacific to the American lodestar. The smaller insular communities cannot, however, persist in a cultural and political no man's land under modern conditions. Each of the paths open to them may be facilitated or blocked by American power; in consequence, delineation of a clear United States policy toward Pacific peoples remains the region's most pressing question.

The second element in United States responsibility is our preference (ourselves eliminated for lack of cultural tolerance) among the several contenders for the role of organizer of the Pacific peoples. Obviously we are not prepared to accept the imperium of Communist China, and Japan's ambitions received an emphatic veto hardly likely to be reversed for several decades. Outmoded colonialism vitiates the possibility of continued rule by European associates; in the Western-style democracies of Australia and New Zealand, racial exclusiveness almost equals our own levels of intolerance. An evasion of political, economic, and cultural responsibility for the development of peoples sheltered by American military might has been the United States grand design in the Pacific since the close of the Japanese war. Growing indications of the failure of an intervention policy among peninsular countries of the Asiatic land mass has brought into sharp relief a policy lacuna affecting Western bases of power and influence in the Pacific realm. American neglect of underlying political factors has stimulated European reassertions of exclusive interests that they had enjoyed throughout the period of colonial dominance. Britain, for example, by unilaterally championing a Malaysian federation committed the United States to an equivocal position concerning the political future of peoples of Malay origin; this has had serious consequences on our relations with Indonesia and the Philippine Republic.

Military engagements, such as SEATO and ANZUS, that were originally intended to control communism and check Japan have been manipulated into channels that were not foreseen by American statesmanship. France has remained aloof from Western commitments, compensating for her diminished power through closer cultural ties with her island territories and with elements in her former area of influence in Indochina. The extent of her divergence from American policies increases as United States difficulties accumulate on the mainland. The Netherlands, naturally bitter from unsympathetic treatment accorded her established interests in the East Indies, is tempted to use her traditional knowledge of the region to exploit Anglo-American difficulties to her own commercial advantage. This disarray of Western interests and policies is made possible, at least in part, by the power umbrella provided by the Seventh Fleet. Strength without purpose invites low-level political maneuvering. As the United States is first in effective power in the Pacific realm, its obligations for the coordination of Western policy appear inescapable. It is only by assuming that neither Communist China nor Soviet Russia constitutes a serious challenge that continuing Western disunity can be tolerated.

France's views on the Pacific are seldom clear to Anglo-

Saxon eyes. Yet De Gaulle's impatience with the monolithic assumptions of the English-speaking cultural complex has certain justifications. Historic France made great investments of her national spirit and energy in an expansion into Asia and the Pacific. Though the gamble of sea power was lost to the Anglo-Saxons, France retained a claim to participate in Pacific and Asian affairs on approximately equal terms with her European rivals until the American broom swept colonial rule into discard along with its usurper, Japanese imperialism. Loss of Cochin China struck bitter roots in the political structure of metropolitan France, aggravating, if not causing, the long agony of the Algerian war. Military and political power are no longer bases for French influence throughout the world; culture, however, understood as a complex of spiritual, intellectual, and institutional attitudes, remains as a fundamental link justifying, in French eyes, a continued special relationship with peoples of former association. A hard core of cultural ties resides in the acceptance of the French language, its inherent pattern of logic, its educational and value assumptions, as a major instrument of world communication. The replacement of French authority by English-speaking peoples threatens to sever these final ties and reduce France's historic investment in the area to a total loss. De Gaulle's France instinctively resists Anglo-Saxon hegemony; it downgrades the communist threat in the face of a more immediate and familiar menace.

In order to assimilate island dwellers of her Pacific territories as fully as practicable to the metropolitan culture, France has adopted an aloof attitude toward Anglo-American projects for the common development of the South

Seas peoples. In the internal politics of North and South Vietnam, France relies on a residual empathy between the indigenous elite and the French institutional and intellectual patterns left from the colonial period to pursue a policy disassociated from the overall designs of her Western partners. The reconciliation of French, American, and British policy, even though it may require a reappraisal of French claims for joint participation in certain spheres of influence, appears a necessity for American statesmanship.

Australia's key position as Western representative in the Pacific realm adds a further dimension to United States power and responsibility. Through air and sea strength, the United States is, in fact, guarantor of the military security of the Australian continent and, by implication, of the long-established "White Australia" policy aimed at the exclusion of Asians. Though the military alliance of ANZUS—from which the United Kingdom was pointedly excluded—was originally framed to cover only Japanese and communist aggression, its extension to threats from Indonesia or elsewhere has become in practice inevitable. Accordingly, the American government finds itself committed to underwriting international policies it has not originated and over which it exercises slight control. By virtue of its rule over New Guinea and Papua, the Commonwealth of Australia may be regarded as the last major colonial power in the Pacific realm. As a natural trade and communication center for far-flung Pacific peoples, her attitude toward potential political or economic confederations is of major moment. Consequently, a traditional clinging to ethnic exclusiveness places Australia in juxtaposition with the Republic of South Africa in the eyes of the bulk of Asian and African nations—Australia's voting record on South African issues in the United Nations provides substance for this suspicion.

Confronting the United States is the establishment of a realistic relationship with Australia in Pacific affairs that will reflect relative strengths and responsibilities. Determining a positive policy to encompass all Western interests in the Pacific realm must be a joint endeavor requiring United States leadership proportionate to our capacity for implementation. Australian-American relations may be stabilized only within the wider framework of such a policy.

Powerful arguments favoring American assumption of political leadership to match its military superiority in the Pacific realm falter at the threshold of specific plans of action; imposition of United States views solely through superior might threatens the coherence of any Western consortium. Fortunately, the pattern of Western policy making is sufficiently flexible to permit consensual planning and direction of international policies, provided the objectives of all participants have been determined and a realistic appraisal undertaken of the facts of the situation. In both these regards the Western alliance has failed to fulfill basic requirements of cohesion in the Pacific area; though United States initiative has fallen woefully short, it is also true that former colonial powers have muddied the waters of Western unity through a lack of candor and an obstinate adherence to the competitive rivalries of a vanished era. Communist China and Indonesia have now sketched out possible alternatives for the future of the region that leave the West no substantial part to play, except as a sterile military intruder serving to inflame further outbursts of Asian nationalism. Defense of Western interests in the Pacific realm must start with a formulation of a policy that is not based on either European or American nationalism exclusively but is primarily Western in outlook. A review of the total situation from a Western rather than a nationalist approach, therefore, might serve as a useful preliminary to the construction of such a policy.

3 • THE CHARACTER
OF BRITISH INTERESTS

Loss of rule and power in the Indian and Pacific oceans altered the direction of British policies, but it left unchanged a basic objective to preserve and develop a profitable link between the economies of the West and the Orient. For a hundred years and more, Britain had been in an advantageous position to dictate the terms of such commerce; now it has to negotiate with equal and even superior political and military entities to accomplish its ends. The broad aim of linking Asia with the Western world is shared with varying degrees of enthusiasm by all noncommunist nations; points of issue, however, arise on the terms of cooperation, including the locus of leadership, the just balance of commercial profit, and joint responsibility for world policy. The involvement of British national interests in all these matters gives rise to particular policies directed toward a British-oriented solution. Though immediate diplomatic and economic actions reflect contingencies of a situation over which Britain retains impaired control, a unique pattern may be traced in overall British policy centered around two continuing concepts that may be characterized as those of Commonwealth and empire.

The fact of Commonwealth membership, though confusing even to the British themselves, carries the heritage of past endeavors into a relationship of continuing endurance. An evaluation sponsored in 1963 by the United Kingdom Commonwealth Relations Office suggests the following rationale:

> The Commonwealth sits astride the world problem of the developed and under-developed nations. To some extent these are the haves and have-nots. The Commonwealth therefore represents one means by which this huge problem can be tackled, and for Britain it represents perhaps the best means. The Commonwealth does still possess a vitality of its own in terms of personal ties, trade and professional links, and close contact and consultation between governments.[1]

A key phrase in this description, "for Britain it represents perhaps the best means," underlines a devisive element that sets the Commonwealth apart from a unified Western approach to Asian and Pacific problems. The special relationship vital to the Commonwealth idea cushions the United Kingdom from some of the harsh realities consequent to the fading of power and empire and increases its reluctance to accept the role of a junior partner in a wider Western association. Justification in some measure exists through the lack of positive Western policy guided and implemented by the United States as the leading Western power in the region. To surrender any of the delicately balanced networks still encompassing areas of previous British rule before a final determination of the United Kingdom's status in the international hierarchy would be considered foolhardy. In practice, the Commonwealth in Asian and Pacific regions is a political channel of communication that facilitates continuous discussion between the regional lands themselves, with the former metropolis, Canada, and important sections of independent Africa. Though the United Nations overrides the Commonwealth as a meeting place of nations, its machinery for discussion and consultation is clumsier, and it can be crystallized for easy association only imperfectly. It may be claimed that the outlook and interests of Commonwealth countries is so disparate that all their instruments of consultation fail to produce meaningful agreements. In questions of specific policies to meet current situations, it is evident that no common foreign policy is likely to arise from the Commonwealth relationship, which remains based on national self-interest. However, the first decade of the new Commonwealth (enriched by newly independent African and Asian members) has indicated that it is capable of significant agreement and action on world issues above the level of diplomatic policy. The present Commonwealth is an institutional monument to the principle of racial equality. When the Republic of South Africa offered a threat to the continuance of the Commonwealth as a wide association of diverse cultures, the United Kingdom and the older dominions affirmed adherence to the principle of racial equality even at the cost of the loss of an important economic associate. The implications of this action for Australia, New Zealand, Canada, and the United Kingdom are far-reaching, and their commitment may be credited as a triumph for the Commonwealth bond.

As an instrument of economic self-interest, the Commonwealth retains some value to the United Kingdom and other members. Intra-Commonwealth trade accounts for about one-third the total quantity of British trade, and the corresponding fraction for all Commonwealth countries taken together is about the same.[2] Whether or not it would be more profitable in the long run for Britain and other members to loosen Commonwealth trading ties in favor of wider associations remains controversial. As an existing arrangement, Commonwealth preferences in all their forms constitute an area of interest to the United Kingdom, a concern shared by the politically diverse communities of India, Australia, Malaysia, and New Zealand. Three major factors underlie the special economic relationships between members of the Commonwealth: trade both on a preferential and natural basis in respect to tropical foodstuffs and basic raw materials; sterling area arrangements encouraging direct financial investment from the United Kingdom; and technical and financial aid provided by the developed to less-developed members.

In the first category of trade in tropical foodstuffs and raw materials, Commonwealth membership inclines the United Kingdom to champion the stabilization of commodity prices. This question touches on one of the great background issues of the modern world—the justice of existing patterns of exchange between technological and nontechnological communities. Britain's measure of commitment, under Commonwealth influence, to the cause of producers of raw materials may create divergence between its world economic policies and those of the United States. The sterling area is primarily a piece of banking machinery that interacts rather than coincides with Commonwealth membership. It does, however, affect the flow of direct capital investment to certain countries in the Pacific realm in favor of the United Kingdom. Though this may prove transitory, an immediate result has been to close a lacuna in these areas that might have provoked a flow of United States capital and led to a consequent shift in economic and political dependency. As a major instrument for the provision of financial aid between developed and less-developed lands, the Commonwealth is inadequate because the ratio of needy to rich countries is too high and also because the United Kingdom is comparatively weak as the main contributor. However, the future of direct financial aid as a means of establishing world economic justice becomes increasingly uncertain. Technical aid, on the other hand, carries with it some of the humanistic vitality underlying the American concept of the Peace Corps. In this sphere, the Commonwealth provides opportunities for the United Kingdom, which were lucidly summarized by a contributor to the Commonwealth Relations Office Conference of 1963:

> Technical assistance means the supply of know-how from one country to another, the supply of experts and skilled personnel, advisers, training equipment, surveys and the provision of scientific advice. It includes education. The Commonwealth is a peculiarly suitable machinery to organize such assistance. It can be effective precisely because of the cultural, institutional and intangible ties that already exist between Britain and Commonwealth countries. There is, too, on the part of the majority of Commonwealth countries a strong desire to make use of

British methods, which are held in high esteem and this cuts right across any political difference that may exist. . . . In technical assistance the Commonwealth has a most valuable part to play in the modern world, both by reason of its functional efficiency and also as something of significance in our emotional lives. In the development of the under-developed parts of the Commonwealth—and the bulk of the Commonwealth is under-developed—we have a purpose for which the Commonwealth structure is particularly well suited. To some extent the loss of an Empire has made British people uncertain where they belong and where their mission in the world lies. The Commonwealth as an association of widely differing States fully recognizes the obligations that exist between richer and poorer countries for mutual understanding and help, and it is to the advantage of everyone that this feeling should be exploited to the full.[3]

Continuity of British cultural and institutional patterns in former possessions in the Pacific realm, then, remains a major United Kingdom interest to be implemented by every means at the nation's command. No less than the French, the British are reluctant to dispose of a historic investment of national spirit and energy that has created over the centuries a special relationship with peoples of Asia and the Pacific. To the United Kingdom, the Commonwealth represents a consensual approach to an adjustment of this historic relationship to conditions of political independence and cultural equality. Preservation of the Commonwealth may complicate the assumption of United States leadership of Western policy in the region. The Commonwealth in the Pacific and Indian oceans, however, lacks inherent force to stand on its own feet against the rest of the world.

Integration with the superior might of the United States is essential to the survival of its component members and therefore dictates general compliance with American interests and policies. Britain, nevertheless, requires recognition of the reality of Commonwealth ties as a condition for acceptance of American leadership.

The second base for special British interests lies in the vestiges of empire. They partly overlap the new Commonwealth but are a sole United Kingdom responsibility that is costly to the British in money and in the disposition of military force. The controversial merger of the former colonies of North Borneo (now Sabah) and Sarawak along with Singapore in the state of Malaysia exemplifies the remaining problems of empire. There are others as potentially disturbing. Fiji is a land divided against itself with Britain as uneasy arbiter. South Sea island peoples are awakening to technology and casting around for political forms that will ensure cultural dignity and economic growth; the initiative in planning suitable groupings, federal or confederate, rests for the moment primarily in British hands. Colonial responsibility has not been abrogated in the Pacific realm though its direction has been changed from possessive imperialism toward a wider harmony of interests between indigenous peoples and Western culture. The formulation and implementation of policies for this purpose constitute a specific British interest engaging both traditional political skills and deployment of economic resources. The administrative authority of the United Kingdom is now and will be for the immediately foreseeable future a potent factor determining the destiny of Pacific peoples.

The remaining colonial possessions of the United Kingdom in the Western Pacific consist of the Fiji Islands, the British Solomon Islands' Protectorate, the Gilbert and Ellice Islands colony, the New Hebrides (under a Franco-British condominium form of rule), Pitcairn Island, and the protected Kingdom of Tonga. A measure of administrative centralization is achieved through the office of the High Commissioner of the Western Pacific, who bears responsibility for general policy in the British Solomons, the Gilbert and Ellice groupings, and the New Hebrides condominium. Fiji as the largest and most important unit among the island possessions retains administrative autonomy under its own Governor, who also exercises supervision over the Tonga protectorate and Pitcairn—until 1951, the Governor of Fiji was also High Commissioner of the Western Pacific, administering the whole region from the Fijian capital at Suva. Removal of the High Commissioner's headquarters to Honiara in the Solomons and separation of the two offices indicated increasing attention to political participation by indigenous communities.

The Fiji Island chain of 300 islands covering a land area of about 7,000 square miles is centered in two main islands, Vita Levu and Vanua Levu. A deep-water port at Suva, the capital, and an international airport at Nadi in the southwest make Vita Levu a traffic center in the South Pacific. The islands possess a tropical economy based on copra and sugar. Attainment of social unity is a major problem that is aggravated by the fact that the original inhabitants are being outnumbered by descendants of immigrants from India—of a total population of approximately 500,000 the 1966 census allocated 235,000 to Indian stock against a Fijian total of 200,000. Europeans numbered 11,000, Chinese 6,000, and peoples from other Pacific islands made up the rest. Accordingly, colonial government concerns itself for the most part with the maintenance of a political and legal order that will give time for an eventual reconciliation of the diverse cultural standards and objectives of the two main groups. Postponement, if not paralysis, of political progress toward self-government and national unity is a price that must be paid for this particular manifestation of the Pax Britannica.

Alternatives, however, present problems involving international implications. Should civil strife arise from political tensions, both sides would be tempted to seek allies in non-Western areas, thus endangering a communication center vital to Western influence in the Pacific and imperiling the Western connection with Micronesian and Polynesian peoples. Indonesia might champion the cause of indigenous Pacific peoples against Indian immigrant stock and a failing colonial rule. On the other hand, the Indian majority, if it failed to obtain active support from its former motherland, could threaten to align itself with Chinese communism along Castroite lines. Australia would find intolerable a threat to vital communications with North America perpetrated by either Indonesia or Red China. In potential circumstances of this character, Britain's interest in control of Fiji transcends mere retention of a colonial possession—her influence and responsibility throughout the Pacific realm is engaged in providing a favorable political solution to the Fijian question. In this matter, the United Kingdom assumes a primary role with her initiative in no way subordinated to the superior power balance of the United States.

Social politics in Fiji revolve around a perennial land

question. Though the economy of the country is dominated by Indian enterprise and labor, particularly the export crop of sugar, ownership of the bulk of the land— slightly over 83 percent—is in Fijian hands. This state of affairs dates from a Deed of Cession entered into in 1874 between the British government and the indigenous rulers that pledged that Fijian land should be inalienable to non-Fijians. As recently as 1959, a British-appointed commission declared that it was "quite impossible to ignore the Fijian right to the ownership of all land in the colony other than Crown land and land under freehold." [4] A Native Land Trust Board, with a majority of Fijian members, controls the disposition of Fijian land along traditional and partly communal lines. Though the value to the economy as a whole of the Indians' contributions is considerably greater than that of the Fijians' and the Indian population increase is 44.75 per thousand as against a Fijian figure of 36.9, Indians are denied access to land essential to their own and the country's economic advancement. Absence of social assimilation, partly due to the exclusiveness of Fijian culture, aggravates a situation that has now become the dominant political issue of the islands. Britain's guardianship of the Fijian element is rooted in historical good faith and in its role as protector of Micronesian and Polynesian peoples over a wider area. Originally, the principle of the Deed of Cession remedied wrongs committed by European land grabbers and provided for the development of a stable native community on its own terms. Economic needs, however, provoked by the lethargy of the Fijians led to the introduction of Indian immigrant labor; the sugar economy on which the material development of the islands depends is almost wholly in the hands of Indian labor and enterprise combined with European (or, more strictly, Australian) capital.

The dilemma of British rule is that it has assumed the nature of a barrier against the economic progress of a majority of the inhabitants, though it protects the cultural autonomy of the indigenous minority. A riotous strike by Indian cane farmers in 1960 dramatized underlying tensions. Though ostensibly directed against the Australian-owned Colonial Sugar Refining Company—since 1926 the sole manufacturer of sugar in Fiji—it exposed generalized feelings of economic exploitation current among the Indian community. The government's response, the creation of a Sugar Marketing Board, indirectly raised the question of the use to which land was being put in relation to the whole economy of the country.

British policy may be said to have reached dead center in Fiji and, by extrapolation, in the whole South Sea island system under United Kingdom control. An administratively convenient policy aimed at preserving the cultural status quo of the islanders has been overtaken by the rapid spread of technology. If colonial government fails to provide opportunities for advancement comparable to those being attempted on the Asian mainland, Melanesian, Micronesian, and Polynesian peoples may turn from partnership with the West to listen to the ancient blood call of Malay culture. The likelihood that Indonesia may usurp the role of protagonist of Malay unity presents a major challenge to Western influence in the Pacific.

The weight of colonial tradition obscures the naked issues at stake throughout the Pacific realm; though benevolent paternalism has worked well in the past the exercise of external political power to preserve archaic cultural frameworks now forms a major obstacle to improvement of living standards through the application of available technology. Cultural change requires that internal sources of energy be freed to experiment and discover new patterns acceptable in time to the whole community. Politics is one of the principal instruments through which peoples engage in social discussion (frequently turbulent) in order to achieve consensual solutions concerning change; unfortunately, legal and traditional order suffers under conditions of live political debate, and this renders the process difficult to reconcile with administrative efficiency. Colonial administrators therefore require firm policy direction from their metropolis to enable them to make adjustments in the established system; they must loosen their authority and thereby stimulate the indigenous people to direct their own affairs. Despite the diversity of cultural situations influencing the vision of the administrator on the ground, island peoples of the Pacific under British rule constitute an entity for the purpose of policy formation on the metropolitan level. A choice exists between rear guard action to maintain a cultural status quo and forward-looking policies aimed at anticipating the inevitable cultural change that is sparked by advancing technology. Political development is the chosen British instrument for the advancement of dependent peoples; the future of Britain in the Pacific lies in a successful ordering of this sphere of activity.

In the key area of Fiji, British administration has established a pattern that may provide a testing ground for relations between Pacific island and Western peoples in general. Nowhere else has the principle of autonomous cultural control been applied with greater administrative and political skill to create a situation that exposes the limitations as well as the values of isolated cultural autonomy under modern conditions. Before scrutinizing the inherent defects of this situation, we should evaluate its achievements. In the first place, the Fijian community has been united as never before in its past history and now lives peaceably under an order that gives continuity to its ancient traditions. This has been brought about by British rule; an orderly union had to be created before the area could be adapted to the spread of technology. The political structure that made this Fijian cultural autonomy possible is sufficiently flexible so that it could, if skillfully directed, be applied to broader purposes.

In place of representative government interpreted in terms of majority rule, communal control has dominated the Fijian scene since 1945. Normally, in a British-administered colony, a legislative council evolves into a popular assembly capable of assuming powers of self-government; here this process was distorted in favor of the communal claims of the Fijian minority. Communal instead of numerical representation dictates the composition of the Legislative Council (four European, four Fijian, and four Indian members). Direct election to the council was practiced only by the Indian and European communities until March, 1962, when the Fijians relinquished a complicated form of indirect elections, chiefly through councils, in favor of the more popular method. A legislative council thus constituted is an imperfect expression of political nationalism and leaves the burden of government to the administrative apparatus of the British-appointed executive. In the case of the Fijians, however, special provisions exist for determining and implementing the administrative policies by the customary leaders of their community. An outstanding Fijian chief, the late Ratu Sir Lala Sakuna, was the principal architect of the system inaugurated in its present form in 1945.

Communal government received official status through the creation of the Fijian Affairs Board, composed of Fijian members of the Legislative Council and headed by the Secretary for Fijian Affairs, a minister in the colonial hierarchy, ex officio member of both Executive and Legislative Councils. Since Sakuna's tenure of this office (1945–1954), the position has been held by British officials aided by a Fijian deputy of chieftain rank. The overwhelming importance of this board is that it is empowered to make regulations—in plain terms legislate—for the bulk of the customary rights and duties that make up the life of the Fijian community. Sakuna, himself a member of the English bar, inspired the compilation of Fijian custom into written terms following the precedent of English common law. In consequence, Fijians live under systems of law and administration that tend to separate them from the majority of Indian descent. Though the Fijian Affairs Board is granted a practical veto over legislation concerning the regulation of Fijian communities that might be placed before the full Legislative Council, its true power rests in the executive and administrative fields, where it serves as the apex of a pyramid of hierarchic and traditional controls over the daily life of the Fijian individual. The Council of Chiefs, a long-established center of the traditional society, retains great influence as an advisory body. On a more practical working level, provincial and district councils formulate orders affecting such matters as communal services to be performed by village inhabitants. The principal executive officers at each level—province, district, and village—are Fijians selected in accordance with customary social patterns; Fijian police enforce regulations, and Fijian magistrates sit in provincial and district courts to interpret customary law.

Though the program Sakuna devised for communal self-government has served to protect a Fijian "way of life," certain artificial elements characterize it as a transitory solution to the wider problems of the area. In the first place, it depends too heavily on the continuance of British colonial rule as a counterweight to an energetic Indian majority; in the second place, it hinders a realistic examination of the economic problem of the use of land sequestered in the hands of Fijian traditional groups; and, finally, it remains questionable to what extent the program permits a majority of the Fijians themselves to participate in controlling their own affairs. Though the maze of elite and elected personnel serving as power centers in Fijian society is fairly impenetrable to the outside observer, it is clear that the dynamic evolution Sakuna expected of traditional village society has not been promoted by the system he devised. Technological change has made inroads of unknown depth among these politically static communities, leaving uncertain the true direction of Fijian commoners' loyalties. Participation by Fijian workers along with Indians in riotous strikes at Suva in 1960 indicates that at least in the well-populated urban center the old order is breaking down. Acceptance of direct election of Fijian members to the Legislative Council in 1962, in place of a complicated process of choice through traditional councils, further denigrated the authority of the chiefs.

In the fall of 1966 elections for a thirty-four seat Legislative Council were held under a revised constitutional plan. Though the principle of ethnic representation was maintained, concessions were made towards implementation of a common roll vote. Nine of the thirty-four seats were filled by cross voting, which ostensibly ignored ethnic lines. The results were disappointing; candidates in the cross voting districts were returned on a strictly racial basis. The most significant result of the 1966 election was the creation of a multiparty structure. The Alliance for All Party, controlled by the Fijian Association under the leadership of Ratu Mara, a man of Fijian kingly stock, won twenty-five out of the thirty-four seats. The Indian Federation Party, led by A. D. Patel, declared itself in favor of independence and majority rule based on the principle of one man one vote. The Europeans and the Chinese (recently enfranchised) associated themselves with the Fijian Alliance to counter the threat of Indian political domination. The support accorded a splinter party, the National Democratic Party, led by a Fijian, Apesai Tora, as well as the election of several independent candidates further complicated the political scene. None of the protagonists appear to have the power to achieve their announced objectives through their own efforts. On the other hand there is little evidence of willingness to push the issues which divide the parties to the point of creating civil disorder. Accordingly, the British remain, perhaps reluctantly, as arbiters. However a growing danger of intervention by external forces reduces the time remaining for a gradual adjustment of the ethnic issues.

In December, 1966, the Fourth Committee of the General Assembly of the United Nations recommended a draft resolution[5] censuring the United Kingdom for not proclaiming an early date for Fijian independence. Further, the resolution supported the Indian residents' demands for general suffrage based on one man one vote. It was also proposed that the General Assembly send a committee to Fiji to study conditions there. This partisan intervention into internal Fijian politics on the part of the world organization was sponsored by Asian-African members supported by communist nations and some Latin American countries. On the final vote only Australia, New Zealand, Portugal, Togo, the United Kingdom, and the United States opposed the resolution. Accordingly Indonesia, Singapore, and the Philippines, under the leadership of India, were able to assert a claim on the determination of the destiny of the neighboring Fijians.

Unless they can align themselves along political and economic lines with kindred Pacific peoples, Fijians face insuperable problems in preserving their ancient culture against the onslaughts on their economy that will be made by modern technology. The presence of an Indian majority in their country that is motivated by economic as opposed to traditional interests reduces the time available for the adaptation of Fijian culture. Britain has responsibility to both its own interests and Western security in general to provide a political framework for this wider association of Pacific peoples, by utilizing the inevitability of technological change to reconcile the cultural gaps between immigrant and indigenous groups. As suzerain over a diversity of evolving societies in the Pacific islands, the United Kingdom is in a position to devise patterns of economic and political association that may win the consent of the separate regions. An illustration of what may be accomplished in a minor key is the successful establishment under Fijian auspices of a training center for indigenous medical practitioners (who have somewhat less preparation than Western physicians) to meet urgent necessities of island communities throughout the whole British and Australian area. The Central Medical School at Suva, generously aided by the Rockefeller Institute, illustrates the scope of practical benefits possible when Western social standards are implemented by joint action of administrative and private skills across nationalist lines.

Colonial responsibility lacks a practical alternative in the case of the British Protectorate of the Solomon Islands. A population of approximately 114,000, mainly Melanesian, is concentrated in the coastal areas of eight large and numerous small islands covering 11,500 square miles of land, 90 percent of which is forest. Undeveloped and naturally difficult physical communications restrict social organization to an extended clan system. Though traditional outlets for aggression through headhunting and intervillage raiding have been suppressed by European intervention, the inhabitants would be prey to sophisticated intruders bearing the gun—the symbol of higher culture—if deprived of the protection afforded by responsible government. That this protection should remain nationalist-colonial indicates an archaic weakness. In the absence of a true policy guiding Western interests in the Pacific, the situation remains governed by historic and geographic considerations; by outmaneuvering European rivals in the nineteenth and early twentieth centuries, Britain ensured that she would be paramount, but she can no longer support this role with effective power. Admitting that the alternatives to European rule would be Indonesian or even Communist Chinese guardianship fails to resolve the question of whether final responsibility should lie in United Kingdom hands or in those of a collective Western group. A United Nations trusteeship has become unacceptable to Britain because the composition of that body favors a majority of newly independent Asian and African states. Though Western control is at present unchallenged, claims to continued guardianship are compromised by a national colonial base that hampers opportunities for economic and social development that might flow from the combined surplus skills and capital of Western countries. The illusion of national exclusiveness, an illusion because it is no longer substantiated by effective power except in the case of the United States, is a malaise that enervates Western influence throughout the whole Pacific realm.

The foremost task confronting Western culture in the Solomons is the creation of a community out of separated village groups that lack physical communication and speak a confusion of dialects. Though common ethnic origins, social attitudes, and like dependence on primitive forms of subsistence agriculture favor union, factors operating against it are of depressing magnitude. Motivations that might drive individual Solomon islanders to abandon traditional ways in order to achieve a wider society are too often seen through Western spectacles. From our perspective, it appears clear that advancing technology will alter the physical environment in such a manner as to render impracticable the previous social order. In the historic past, however, similar situations resulted for the most part in the imposition of another form of order on an essentially passive population by superior external force. If Islamic Indonesia or Communist China were to replace European colonial powers, compulsory assimilation of the islanders into the metropolitan cultural pattern would constitute an unhesitating aim. Western peoples' belief in the universal validity of their culture patterns lacks equal vigor, perhaps on account of the cost involved in a general sharing of economic standards among the bulk of the world's inhabitants. The Western objective in the islands, then, remains equivocal; our domestic standards appear unsuitable for export to impoverished exotic climes. Britain, for her own convenience and out of innate national habit, has imposed order on indigenous societies without providing any clear sense of direction. Once the imperial dream—always a minority fantasy in the homeland—was eclipsed by a shift in power realities, total responsibility for the guidance of alien and distant culture groups became an embarrassment that was unconvincingly cloaked by pious good will. Abandonment of unprofitable colonial dependencies would relieve both the conscience and the pocket of the British taxpayer, if reasonable hope existed that they would stay abandoned and not fall prey to expanding systems of economic and political rivals. In existing circumstances, the United Kingdom cannot be expected to accomplish more than a holding operation until the collective mind of the West becomes clear on the conditions of its relations with less-organized peoples on an immature technical level; if assimilation to our way of life on equal terms is impracticable and undesirable, what form of guidance should stem from our unquestioned power?

Isolated from the ferment among independent Asian and Malayan peoples by the "no trespassing" sign of European colonialism, the Melanesians of the Solomons have been relieved from certain past miseries without gaining noticeable impetus into the new world of technology. The precarious link that their economy, based on subsistence agriculture and the export of copra, affords with the world of technical skills is insufficient for social improvement at more than a snail's pace. Vigorous development of timber resources and perhaps unsurveyed mineral wealth is an obvious possibility in effecting a breakthrough to economic growth. Whether the Western method of capitalist enterprise or the mass socialism of emerging Asia is adopted, mobilization of indigenous labor into paid employment on an increasing scale appears inevitable. In 1956, only 6,000 of the 114,000 indigenous inhabitants looked to paid employment for their livelihood. The question at issue resolves itself into a choice of political systems, a Western order that will motivate individuals along lines of self-betterment or a socialist complex functioning on group discipline. Power and will are more likely to prove to be the determinants than theoretical desirability, and the West as tenant in possession will surrender, if at all, by default. Consent of the inhabitants, not yet a nation or a true community, to whatever system is imposed from outside can hardly be expressed in advance but should be judged by the degree of participation accorded each progressive step.

The pattern of colonial government reestablished after the ravages of the Japanese war favors participation by the Solomon islanders in the conduct of their own affairs. Though central government remains firmly in the hands of British administrators, native councils, some of which are islandwide, have engaged in developing social services in their areas, coordinating their efforts with more sophisticated means contributed by government and religious missions. Since 1954, local native councils have been empowered to prepare finance estimates and levy on all able-bodied males a native tax, at rates varying according to district needs, that is subject to the scrutiny and consent of the central administration. In principle, this should lead in time to the exercise of responsible self-government; there is not enough money available, however, from the local economy to render local governmental processes an effective instrument of social change. The ordinary revenues in 1957 amounted to 569,824 Australian pounds, but bare expenditure requirements were 1,016,613 pounds. Grants from the metropolitan government to the tune of 300,000 Australian pounds covered the deficit. Yet this inadequate financing was achieved with great effort by both the local community and the United Kingdom government, both revenue and expenditure having tripled since 1947. A development plan for economic and social growth is being financed largely from Colonial Development and Welfare funds contributed by the British government.

Economic shifts since the Japanese war are encouraging self-reliance among the islanders; the plantation economy is dwindling and copra production is now almost wholly in native hands. A copra board, established after the war, buys all copra produced outside the plantations and markets it under a governmental agreement with Unilever in London. The cultivation of cocoa by islanders themselves is making headway against a plantation-grown product. Alienation of land to nonindigenous owners has been prohibited since 1914; before that date, some 400,000 acres out of an approximate 7,000,000 occupied acres had passed into the possession of European planters. The potentially important timber industry is monopolized by two large companies producing more for export than domestic consumption.

The attitude of the Solomon Islanders toward gradual

absorption in the Western technical complex may be regarded as foreshadowing some of the major problems of the West in its relations to emerging cultures in the Pacific realm. In the first place, the nefarious Labor Trade, a form of deceitful abduction and even plain kidnapping to meet labor needs in Queensland and elsewhere, created a pattern of contact between Europeans and islanders that was based on callous exploitation and murderous response. Though the practice was outlawed for all British subjects and vessels in the South Seas by an Order in Council issued in 1877, racist feelings were implanted. Next, the Japanese invasion, followed by the American counterinvasion in which the British played a negligible part, confused the inhabitants on the nature of Western protection. An interesting political consequence was the Marching Society movement that started on the island of Malaita during the war and spread throughout the protectorate. Essentially this was a self-help movement preaching noncooperation with government and missionary societies. Though at the start it evoked skilled native leadership advocating improved agriculture and congregation in larger settlements, the emotional appeal centered around an impossible myth of an earthly paradise in which all Europeans would leave, but their goods would continue to arrive through magical means arranged by the islanders' dead ancestors. This economics of superstition betrayed a psychological inability on the part of the islanders to face a slow and strenuous climb to the enjoyment of the fruits of modern technology. A certain paralysis of will has resulted that hinders cooperation between the indigenous island councils and British administrators. Improvement in intra- and interisland communication resulting from wartime activities—Guadalcanal, for example, possesses thirty-five miles of American-built paved roads—has broken down parochialism and created a political consciousness on a wider community scale. This growth of island nationalism reduces the time available for the reconciliation of Melanesian and Western modes of life and opens potential gateways for the intrusion of rival systems. The encouragement and guidance of indigenous political leadership will be exceptionally difficult for colonial administration unless an overriding policy of political advancement is imposed by the metropolitan government. Lacking strong motivations along either cultural or trade lines, the United Kingdom is unlikely to provide imaginative solutions until it is faced with a dangerous degree of alienation among the islanders.

A hopeful achievement is the growth of literacy, now reported at 80 percent. Though elementary education is now practically universal, secondary education still lags, and higher education is just being started. In the political field a revised constitution inaugurated in 1964 provides for eight elected members to a twenty-two member Legislative Council. The indigenous voice, however, remains strictly advisory to the authority of the British-controlled Executive Council and High Commissioner.

In contrast with the sullen caution of the Solomon Islanders in face of technological change, the Micronesians of the Gilbert and Ellice Islands manifest an outgoing attitude. Thirty-five scattered coral atolls and islands constituting the group face population pressures that drive a large proportion of their inhabitants to work elsewhere, generally as laborers on plantations or in phosphate mining on Ocean Island. Perhaps because of the dominance of economic concerns, the islanders have achieved a high degree of self-organization through cooperative societies. The destruction of the precarious natural resources during the Japanese war induced the British administration to create a Wholesale Society, which was entrusted with supplying requirements of existing cooperative societies and carrying on any other form of trade, particularly in relation to the export of copra. Now the cooperative societies spread among the islands, together with the Wholesale Society, form the only means of trading throughout the territory. Several societies own their own ships and trucks, and the majority own their own stores. This communal organization of livelihood maintains continuity with the islanders' social traditions. Both the Micronesians and their British administrators welcome the benefits of technical change. The major political question at issue is whether national colonial rule provides the fullest opportunities for economic expansion. Essential imports restricted to British and Australian sources are perhaps relatively expensive. Offsetting these restrictive trade practices, on the other hand, are substantial grants from the United Kingdom Colonial Development and Welfare funds—during the 1946–1955 period, postwar development schemes received grants of 327,000 pounds sterling.

Despite mutual good will on both sides, it does not appear certain or even probable that the Micronesian islanders can obtain a satisfactory foothold within the Western system at the present rate of progress. Though their cooperative system and their willingness to venture abroad provide a framework for the adaptation of capitalist economics, the area of endeavor open is too limited for practical success. As part of an integrated South Seas economy, related on equitable terms to Western finance and technology, the Micronesians could look forward to an expanding culture that would preserve continuity with the past. British colonialism, despite its enlightened benevolence, provides too narrow a base of opportunity. A decision on a permanent alignment for the Micronesian peoples must await the tardy resolve of Western nations as to whether they can achieve a unified Pacific policy in economic and political as well as military terms. National guardianship is an increasingly precarious transitory stage.

One alternative pattern of relationship between the technological masters of the world and remote cultures is illustrated on a miniature scale by the British protectorate of the Kingdom of Tonga. The Tonga, or Friendly, Islands group lying southeast of Fiji is inhabited by around 63,000 Polynesians with a virile history of cultural homogeneity and independence. Contact with Europeans precipitated the formation of a political state under a central government that was ingenious enough to play off the British against the French and Germans and thus secure a measure of control over the destinies of its own people. The pen of a Voltaire would be required to do justice to the fantastic charade of European intrusion; the religious strife between followers of Methodist and Catholic missionaries, the jack-in-the-box appearance of French, German, and British warships bearing contradictory fiats concerning the island's internal affairs, the rule of the arrogant missionary prime minister, and the final triumph of the wise old king. Mainly through a display of stubborn good sense, the Tongans prevailed over the bumbling of the gun-bearing Europeans to a point where the right to manage their own internal affairs was accorded in return for acceptance of the United Kingdom as their protector and spokesman in relation to the rest of the world. The Treaty of Amity between Great Britain and Tonga, negotiated in 1900, preserved the reality of self-government; the British agent was not to interfere in internal affairs or administration, except where the interests of British subjects or foreigners were concerned. In return, the King of Tonga agreed "to have no relations of any sort with foreign Powers," thus establishing a true external protectorate. Because of the unusual terms of this treaty, the United Kingdom does not list Tonga among the non-self-governing territories for which reports must be submitted to the United Nations.

Granted the opportunity to arrange their own social and political structure, the Tongans have chosen of their own accord to follow a Methodist pattern in religion and a monarchical, parliamentary system on the British model in politics. The Tongan Parliament follows closely the rituals practiced at Westminster and the statuesque presence of the island's late Queen at a royal coronation in London evoked enthusiasm from the English public. The Tongan adaptation of Western political values indicates that Pacific peoples on similar cultural levels might well be left to their own devices free from the humiliation of colonial supervision. The pleasing situation of Tonga is based, however, on an artificial isolation from political and economic realities in the surrounding area that limits its development as a people in the world of modern communications. The nature of the "protection" afforded by the British goes beyond defense against external attack; it determines the nature of Tongan economic contacts with the rest of the world. Though admission to the benefits of technological change requires the integration of the Tongan economy in much wider groupings, the nationalist bias of British suzerainty frustrates Tongan attempts to reach out for wider horizons. If the interests of Western security still dictate a measure of control over Pacific peoples, grants of limited self-government provide inadequate compensation for divisive and artificial isolation imposed by Western nationalism.

Pitcairn Island, situated about halfway between New Zealand and South America, lies outside the field of politics. Its 143 inhabitants, mainly descendants of the mutineers of the *Bounty,* earn their livelihood from subsistence agriculture on the two square miles of the island's territory. Education at the single island school is free up to the secondary level, and a medical survey made in 1950 showed the inhabitants to be free of diseases of any kind, with the exception of dental caries. Revenue is obtained almost entirely from the sale of stamps; in 1957, government income amounted to three times its expenditure. This stubborn refuge from technological change, well served with shipping on the United Kingdom-New Zealand sea route, shows a lack of inclination and capacity to engage in the modern world.

The curious governmental system of the New Hebrides —a condominium between France and Great Britain— illustrates the continuing ill effects of past European rivalries. Though the British are minor partners in the economic and social affairs of the territory, they cling to political claims that serve to paralyze political evolution in the islands. An Anglo-French protocol of 1914 governs the status of the inhabitants, principally in terms of guaranteeing equal rights of residence, protection, and trade to subjects and citizens of the two colonial powers. Missionary

societies have been the primary Western influence on the
indigenous culture, proselytizing with a vigor that has led
to anti-European reaction in favor of ancient "customs." As
future trends in this area appear more dependent on
French than British initiative, they will be discussed in a
later chapter.

Continued possession of the overwhelmingly Chinese island of Hong Kong, with its peninsular bridge to the mainland, places the British in the position of discreet door-
keeper to an unacknowledged gateway of trade and contact
between Communist China and the West.[6] For many complicated economic and political reasons, the government of
Red China tolerates a British presence that is no longer
supported by adequate force. Hong Kong illustrates the
triumph of the logic of economics over political theory in
practical affairs. An entrepôt of trade in this area is convenient and valuable to both Chinese and Western interests, provided that it is not turned into an instrument of political warfare. British administration is delicately adjusted
to avoid giving offense to the political sensitivities of the
neighboring colossus, which in turn has a myopic vision of
the imperial enclave on its own shores. Hong Kong flour-
ishes exceedingly in economic well-being despite its existence in a political limbo, indicating that a possible future
may be conceived for modern versions of the Free Cities that
once mediated the turbulence of medieval Europe. Continued control over this vestigial remnant of European occupation of Chinese territory ensures to the British a special relationship to the Communist government of China.
Because Hong Kong is a trading post primarily, rather than
a permanent settlement, for both its British administrators
and its approximately three million inhabitants, the gov-

ernmental structure is subordinated to the management of the economy. Neither racial nor cultural issues assume political form, and aspirations to true self-government appear impracticable under an ever-present threat of occupation by Red China. In any case, the British lease over the land on which Hong Kong is built expires in favor of mainland China within the next thirty years. Accordingly, an archaic pattern of British colonial rule, with a legally supreme governor, assisted by appointed legislative and executive councils, survives as the constitutional form. Local opinion is expressed for the most part through urban councils and by representatives of corporate groupings. Politics, in the American understanding of the term, would appear a meaningless preoccupation to the vast majority of the inhabitants. Administration attains high levels of professional skill and humanity, however, at least within limits set by almost intolerable conditions of overcrowding and the lack of economic opportunity for a burgeoning population.

The core of British interest and responsibility in the Pacific realm is no longer linked to direct colonial administration. The new state of Malaysia in assimilating the previous colonial territories of Singapore, Sarawak, and Sabah relieved the United Kingdom of primary involvement in indigenous affairs. However, a new concept of guardianship, equally burdensome to the United Kingdom, has been devised to meet external threats to the integrity of the Malaysian federation. This is the gravamen of the charge of neocolonialism leveled against the United Kingdom by Indonesia and to a lesser extent the Philippines. The key position of Malaysia in the present situation of the Pacific realm is treated in an ensuing chapter.

Though remaining colonial territories provide only a secondary interest to Britain in the Pacific, formal recognition has been accorded to the need for a unified policy through the creation and functioning of the Western Pacific High Commission. Implementation of common policies, administrative and economic, under central direction would add greatly to opportunities for development among scattered Pacific peoples. Unfortunately, the British framework is too narrow, embracing only the Solomons, Gilbert and Ellice Islands, and New Hebrides with tenuous connections to Fiji and the semi-independent protectorate of Tonga. International accords have to be reached before effective unification of economic and social plans for development become practicable. Within the Commonwealth itself, Australia and the United Kingdom have failed to clarify their respective roles and responsibilities throughout a contiguous area. The need for greater unification of economic and administrative policies affecting the future development of the peoples of New Guinea, Papua, the Solomons, Fiji, the Gilbert and Ellice Islands, and adjacent territories appears subordinated to considerations of national pride and self-interest on the part of the protecting powers. On a broader international scale, the future of the Pacific islanders is compromised by the projection of British, French, and American national interests into the solution of a problem common to all and capable of proper resolution only through unified policies. Goodwill on the administrative level is insufficient to compensate for the failure of the metropolitan governments to clarify their true objectives and to sacrifice petty national claims to the attainment of general Western security in the Pacific realm. Putative instrumentalities for achieving unification already exist in the form of the South Pacific Commission and other international arrangements. The will to implement any imaginative policy of advancement through such bodies, however, remains paralyzed in a web of indifference and nationalistic bickering.

4 • THE MALAYSIAN FEDERATION

Western interests in the Pacific received a sharp challenge when Indonesia confronted the Malaysian Federation. The strategic and commercial interests previously buttressed through colonial domination had achieved satisfactory continuity within the independent Malaya of British creation. Extension of this political framework over the territories of Sabah, Sarawak, and eventually Brunei, together with an acceptable place for the Chinese of Singapore, apparently secured continuing Western control over the Straits of Malacca. Indonesian and Philippine opposition to this resolution of the colonial question was based, for the most part, on a vaguely defined accusation of "neocolonialism." The imprecision of this concept, however, did not lessen the gravity of the threat to Western influence.

A blunter challenge to all forms of established Western

privilege and power throughout the area might have provoked open struggle with American might. Tactical discretion dictated directing hostility against the more vulnerable aspects of British policy. Neocolonialism, as conceived by Sukarno, has significance only as a means of dividing Western associates in their defense of common interests; otherwise it is a synonym for a Western presence in any form. Malaysia, representing a satisfactory reconciliation of Asian and Western interests in the peninsular and insular regions of the Pacific realm, provided a logical focus for attack by proponents of exclusive Pan-Asian ambitions. Malaya, linked with Thailand, is a vital land bastion of Western influence in peninsular Asia—its successful breach might overthrow the whole precarious balance of power both in Asia and throughout the Pacific realm.

Through agreements stemming from colonial days, Malaysia serves as an effective base for British land and sea power in Asia and the Pacific with the concomitant advantage of having her own security relative to neighboring lands guaranteed more by British arms than through her own military potential. With a population of under 10 million, Malaysia accordingly possesses unrealistic weight in her dealings with surrounding states of more impressive manpower; Indonesia claims 95 million inhabitants, and the Philippine Republic and Thailand 27.5 and 26 million respectively. Some justification exists, then, for the Indonesian view that Britain has not withdrawn from her power position in the region through transference of sovereignty to an independent Malaysia but remains as a deciding factor in the power politics of the area. The agreement concluded between the United Kingdom, the Federation of Malaya, North Borneo, Sarawak, and Singapore for the establishment of Malaysia contains eleven brief articles of which the most significant is Article V on the subject of defense:

> The Agreement on External Defence and Mutual Assistance between the Government of the United Kingdom and the Government of the Federation of Malaya of 12th October 1957, and its annexes shall apply to all territories of Malaysia, and any reference in that Agreement shall be deemed to apply to Malaysia, subject to the proviso that the Government of Malaysia will afford to the Government of the United Kingdom the right to continue to maintain the bases and other facilities at present occupied by their Service authorities within the State of Singapore and will permit the Government of the United Kingdom to make such use of these bases and facilities as that Government may consider necessary for the purpose of assisting in the defence of Malaysia, and for Commonwealth defence and for the preservation of peace in South-East Asia.[1]

The exact wording of this agreement is significant because Malaya, after independence, rejected membership in the South East Asia Treaty Organization (SEATO) and its 1957 defense agreement with Britain specifically provided that British bases in the federation would not be used to support hostilities other than those provoked by attacks on British Far Eastern dependencies without express permission from the Malayan government. The vague phrase "as that (British) Government may consider necessary . . . for the preservation of peace in South-East Asia" means that Malaysia could be a base for British operations of almost any military character throughout the Indian and Pacific oceans, at least in the eyes of neighboring countries.

The extent of British military strength not only through the Singapore base but within the whole Malay peninsula affects the power balance between the independent nations of the area. Of the 225 square miles composing Singapore island, approximately 10 percent is occupied by British military establishments that provide civil employment to some 40,000, or roughly 9 percent of Singapore's working population.[2] Use as a marshaling center for sea and air power rather than as a fortress for defense is the true purpose of the Singapore base. The headquarters of the Royal Air Force for the Far East (FEAF) are located at Changi airfield, and two other subsidiary airfields on the island are under its command; an additional air base is located on Penang island, five hundred miles northeast in the Malacca Straits. Britain's Far East Fleet has use of the facilities of the famous Singapore Harbor and also occupies Woodlands Naval Base in the north of the island. An approximate troop strength of 50,000 is maintained at Singapore by the British army.[3] In the Federation of Malaya, proper, the Commonwealth Strategic Reserve, composed of some 10,000 United Kingdom and Australian troops, is stationed at the Malacca Terendak Cantonment. Ghurka troops, still in British service under agreement with the Kingdom of Nepal, are the core of a jungle-trained force for defense of Malaysia's frontiers. Indigenous forces, though augmented under threat of Indonesian confrontation, number little more than 15,000 men for all services. Supplied for the most part from British sources, they are still commanded on the top levels by British and Commonwealth nationals.

The United States has no direct national interest in Malaysia, nor does it have any international obligation arising from treaty agreements; in the language of national diplomacy, Malaysia is a British "responsibility." Unfortunately, realities of power in the region are no longer based on national lines and the Western, or at least Anglo-American, commitment in Asia and the Pacific has become indivisible.

Malaya was nursed into being by the British from traditional nonnational elements that would probably have foundered in the cataclysmic Asia of today without external protection. The conservative society of the Malay sultanates, guided by British officials into the framework of a modern state, enjoyed a leisurely transition into an age of technological upheaval. Popular movements that have given a distinctive character to the structures of the Indonesian and Philippine governments have had slight effect on the placid continuity of Malayan society. Convenience and compromise, together with acceptance of traditional authority, remain the standards of Malayan public life. To Western eyes, such characteristics may appear to be insurance against the revolutionary trends convulsing the region as well as a promise that economic links will continue. Other Asian states, however, particularly Indonesia, view Malayan conservatism as a symptom of undeveloped nationalism; they question whether the country, delicately balanced between Malayan and Chinese elements, is firmly united behind the present form of government. In light of these doubts, they are tempted to subvert the people from loyalty to the present system by spreading inflammatory social ideas that might lead to demands for a wider political union under Indonesian leadership. The formation of Malaysia, involving the absorption of the preponderantly non-Malay peoples of Singapore, Sabah, and Sarawak, provided an opportunity to test the viability of the Malayan nation-state. Despite British and American interest in preserving an autonomous Malaysia, the Indonesian thesis may not be dismissed as mere excuse for aggression. Though on the immediate question of the merger of Sabah and Sarawak in the Malaysian state a British assurance of indigenous consent was verified by a United Nations mission, the long-term loyalties of mixed communal groups—Ibans, Dusuns, Land and Sea Dyaks, Chinese, and Malays—is likely to be determined more by the course of events than through constitutional arrangements. Despite its ramshackle economy, Indonesia constitutes a centripetal force as the largest aggregate of people of Malay origin; it ranks fifth in the population classification of world states. An ideological *élan,* blended from ethnocentrism and socialist authoritarianism, compensates for standards of living that are inferior in most respects to those enjoyed by inhabitants of the Malay peninsula. Opposition groups within Malaysia itself possess, in general, a left-wing character that renders them sympathetic to the type of popular authoritarianism developed by Sukarno under the appellation of "guided democracy." In Malaya proper the Socialist Front, in Singapore the Barisan Socialists, in Sarawak the Sarawak United People's Party, and in Brunei the now banned Partai Rakyat have demonstrated strong opposition to the new federation for reasons based on a reluctance to perpetuate the existing social organization under the guise of Malaysian nationalism.

Western interests dare not commit themselves without reservation to any immediate manifestation of Malaysian politics, whether in the form of national solidarity or revolutionary discontent, for the sufficient reason that it is not practicable to forecast likely changes in the attitude of the bulk of the community toward the form of political union advocated by the present regime. Responsibility for the nature and scope of Asian nationhood should cease with the loosening of the colonial tie—"protected" regimes, however compatible with Western notions, provide a perilous foothold for continuing Western influence in the peripheral lands of the Asian continent. Britain's commitment to a Malaysian regime in the face of Indonesian and Philippine opposition is based more on the special problems surrounding liquidation of a colonial empire than on any accepted Western strategy of relations with the Far East. Because the United Kingdom acts as a participant, disposing of its political real estate to best advantage, her national concerns cloud aspects of broader Western policy.

Though the means by which Malaysia was created and sustained may mark unwise intrusion of Western power in intramural affairs of Pacific peoples, neither Britain nor the West in general has cause to question the worth of the Malayan state as an exemplar of mutually profitable relations between the Orient and Atlantic states. Since independence, the Malayan economy has widened trade ties with the Western complex, maintaining patterns of free enterprise and fiscal self-sufficiency that give it claim to rank among the free peoples. Communal problems that might have wrecked the stability of more experienced nations have been met without provoking racial bigotry or cultural intolerance. The political organization has permitted the expression of popular opinion through representative means without breaching the efficiency of a workable administrative apparatus. By and large, the smooth transition of Malaya from colonial rule to independent self-government has demonstrated the viability of a Western technological and ideological contribution to emergent nations of Asia and the Pacific. The preservation of the Malayan *modus vivendi* is a challenge to the collective statesmanship of the West—a test that will largely fail if met only with force that divorces Malaysia from her sister peoples of Malay origin.

The constitution of Malaysia is modeled, naturally enough, on the structure of the parent Federation of Malaya. To American eyes, the problems of nation building in Malaya appear familiar—the gradual transformation of an association of traditional states, each with its own cultural heritage, into the union of one people. A certain lack of understanding of the meaning of federalism led British officialdom in 1947 to attempt to impose a unitary form of government on the English model as the price of Malayan self-government. The reaction of Malayan public opinion was unexpectedly sharp, and Britain quickly revised its proposals into federal form with a clear division of responsibility between the governments of the federal union and the governments of the eleven component states. In distinguishing spheres of power, the Federation of Malaya Agreement of 1948 granted wider economic and police powers to the central government than are to be found in the eighteenth-century Constitution of the United States. Nevertheless, the constituent states retain important functions in the fields of the development of natural resources and the overseeing of local government bodies. Representative government serves as a basis for popular control through a House of Representatives returned by the electors of single-member constituencies on a majority vote. The Senate reflects an early stage in American constitutional arrangements because most of the senators are chosen by the legislative assemblies of the states. Sixteen of the thirty-eight senators, however, are appointed by the nation's head of state from men of national distinction who are either in the professions or commerce or are representatives of minority ethnic groups.

Citizenship with its concomitant voting rights proved a serious obstacle to the formation of a political framework for an independent Malaya. Communal tension between Malay and Chinese constituents of the population provoked a long-drawn-out struggle to restrict citizenship in favor of indigenous Malays; though final union was accompanied by belated recognition of the citizenship rights for residents of Chinese origin, residual privileges for the Malays were embodied in the constitution. These included acceptance of Malay as the national language, adoption of Islam as the official religion, reservation of a proportionately large number of government service positions for Malays—the head of state, the Yang di-Pertuan Agong, elected by the Malayan sultanate from among their own members, has specific responsibility for safeguarding Malayan interests—and an educational bias in favor of promoting Malayan as the principal indigenous language of instruction.

The Borneo states of Sabah and Sarawak entered the Federation of Malaysia under terms arranged by two governmental bodies, both somewhat remote from indigenous control—the Cobbold Commission, a strictly British body, appeared on the Bornean scene in 1962 and reported that a Federation of Malaysia was in the best interest of North Borneo (now Sabah) and Sarawak; actual terms for the merger were determined by an intergovernmental committee (the Lansdowne Committee)[4] on which British, Malayan, and the colonial regimes of Borneo were represented. Despite the United Kingdom's theoretical right to dispose of colonial possessions at will, the indigenous political parties were fully consulted, and most of their requirements for a voluntary consolidation of their states with Malaya embodied in the final agreement. Accordingly, the new federation is considerably looser than its parent, Malaya, in terms of social union as well as administrative cohesion; to allay a reasonable fear that the former colonial regions might be exploited through the influx of more sophisticated residents from Malaya proper, the constitution granted the component Borneo states control over the entry into their territories of federation citizens as well as aliens. Language and educational and job privileges in favor of Malays will not operate within the new states. In representational terms, the additional states were treated generously, Sabah being accorded sixteen and Sarawak twenty-four seats in the House of Representatives, an allotment that permitted constituencies with half the number of electors customary in Malaya itself. Further, during an initial period of years, representatives from Borneo will be elected by state legislatures and not by direct election as in the rest of the country. It would be fair to presume, then, that the peoples of Borneo, possessing only equivocal ethnic and cultural ties with the peninsular Malays, are being eased into a tenuous union based more on future consent than immediate initiative. Existence of alternative possibilities for the future political alignment of Borneo presents understandable temptations to Indonesia and the Philippines, who believe, with some justice, that present decisions have been taken by British officialdom and not through the clearly expressed will of the inhabitants.

An opportunity for intervention in British Borneo by In-

donesian political factors operating with the support of, if
not officially on behalf of, their government was presented
by a short-lived revolt in Brunei in December, 1962. This
uprising was conducted by Brunei's principal political
party—the Partai Rakyat—which had previously won all
the seats in the first popular elections for district councils,
thereby entitling it to a majority of the nonappointive seats
in the colony's Legislative Council. The party leader,
Azahari, who had fought alongside Sukarno in Indonesia
against the Dutch, tended toward a revolutionary and pro-
Asian outlook. Though his ill-timed rising was speedily
suppressed by British troops, he was able to lay the basis
for guerrilla activities by discontented elements in Sarawak
and Sabah as well as Brunei. As a matter of Indonesian
policy, Sukarno and his Army Chief of Staff, Nastution, en-
couraged this guerrilla-type warfare against the British and
the regime of Tunku Abdul Rahman in Malaya. A flow
of Indonesian arms and "volunteers" to the troubled areas
appeared an inexpensive and relatively safe means of implementing the Sukarno vow to "crush Malaysia." Open
acknowledgment of Indonesian responsibility for subversive activities resulted in a ministerial conference at Bangkok in February, 1964, where the governments of Malaysia, Indonesia, and the Philippines agreed to a cease-fire
arrangement to be supervised by the government of Thailand. This peace-making effort collapsed almost immediately. Tentative intervention in the dispute by the United
States through a visit to Indonesia by the then Attorney
General, Robert Kennedy, acting as emissary of President
Johnson, produced little more than short-lived assurances
by Sukarno that his regime would refrain from open warfare. Guerrilla fighting continued, however, aggravated by

increasingly threatening declarations from the Indonesian government. Small-scale raids on the mainland of Malaya itself, led by Indonesian personnel, provoked the government of Malaysia into bringing a formal charge against Indonesia before the Security Council of the United Nations. In September, 1964, a Soviet veto defeated a resolution deploring Indonesian guerrilla attacks against Malaysia, though nine of the eleven nations composing the council were in favor of the rebuke to Indonesia. The Indonesian government appeared determined to pursue an aggressive policy against Malaysia even in the face of general disapproval of its associates among nonaligned nations in Asia and Africa.

Previous to the formation of Malaysia, some form of union with Malaya had been under consideration by the self-governing colony of Singapore. A stumbling block existed in the reluctance of the Malay states to admit to common citizenship the Singapore Chinese element (1,231,000 out of a total population of 1,634,000).[5] A preponderance of non-Chinese inhabitants in the prospective Borneo states provided an acceptable balance of more than two Chinese to every three members of other constituent groups making up the proposed federation. The ruling faction in the self-governing colony of Singapore negotiated terms of merger that provided for the continuance of the territorial powers of their own legislative body and executive. Popular consent in Singapore to the principle of merger with Malaya was signified through a referendum that recorded 75 percent of the voters in favor, though both the meaning of the question placed before the voters and the manner in which the referendum was conducted were subsequently denounced by opposition groups as tainted with political trickery.[6] Functioning as a main entrepôt of trade in the Pacific and Indian ocean regions, Singapore adapts its political loyalties to commercial advantages. Though trade with Malaya is vital to its prosperity, Indonesian markets may not be dismissed as negligible.

In August, 1965, two factors of internal politics brought about the sudden collapse of the union between Malaysia and Singapore. In the close balance existing between political factions in Singapore, the hostility of the Barisan Socialists to the merger weakened the domestic position of Prime Minister Lee Kuan Yew. In the mainland politics of Malaya, his vigorous participation afforded more strength to the Chinese element than the conservative Malay factions were prepared to accept. Accordingly, Prince Abdul Rahman, Prime Minister of the Malaysian Federation, moved to force the secession of Singapore as a preferable alternative to the outbreak of communal violence.

The appearance of an independent Singapore complicates the defense structure of the Pacific basin for Britain, the United States, and Australia. Though defense agreements permitting the British Far East Command continued use of its Singapore base have been maintained, the security of this base as a linchpin holding together the forces of the United States Pacific Command and British island positions south of India between Africa and Australia is decidedly weakened. In the first place, the regime of Lee Kuan Yew faces the threat of leftist opponents linked by ethnic and cultural ties to Communist China. Second, Lee, himself, has expressed an active interest in redefining the concept of regional defense so as to prevent Singapore from becoming involved in its capacity as a base in the commitments of SEATO. His public utterances have made clear that on no account will his regime permit the substitution of the United States for Britain as occupant of the base.

On occasion the Prime Minister has even referred to a possible request for guardianship of Singapore by the Union of Socialist Soviet Republics, should British protection be withdrawn. This may be evaluated as a rhetorical gesture, at least under existing circumstances, in light of the internal communist opposition to the Lee government.

Western interests as a whole are involved in the degree of support accorded by Britain to Malaysia in its present form; the United Kingdom commitment has entangled the United States and Australia in a general policy for the region that has been inadequately analyzed or evaluated by American opinion. Should one of several possible organizational patterns for peoples of Malay stock be supported by Western military strength in face of opposition from the most highly populated centers of Malay culture? A reasoned answer to this query should take into account whether the fact of association of the major peninsular and insular countries of the Pacific is more important to the West than the form of their association. If Communist China is regarded as the principal adversary of Western interests on a long- as well as short-term basis, then a resolute grouping of peoples of Malay origin offers a more tenable defense line than our present intervention in the internal affairs of independent states of the former Indochina.

Sukarno at one time proclaimed with apparent sincerity that his long-term objective was the creation of a Malay confederation powerful enough to resist military or cultural aggression from either communist or Western sources. Before the Malaysia crisis embittered relations, some progress had been made toward the formation of a consultative council composed of the heads of state to supervise mutual defense plans for Indonesia, the Philippines, and Malaya. The "Manila Declaration" of August, 1963, signed by the leaders of all three governments, embodied the agreement under a confederative nomenclature, Maphilindo. It is significant that the joint statement of the formation of Maphilindo stressed the "temporary nature" of United States military installations in the Philippines and British bases in Malaya.[7] The late President Macapagal of the Philippines had previously declared in an independence day speech to his people, "From here on it should not come as a surprise to any other nation and to the world that the three nations of Malay origin, drawing upon the spiritual strength born of the awareness of their common racial stock and their geographical propinquity, will continue to resolve their common problems in justice and peace." [8] A confederation of the proposed character of Maphilindo would be unlikely to seek close association with the West so long as Indonesia constituted one of its major components; on the other hand, neither the Philippines nor Malaya could be readily forced into the Chinese or Soviet orbit. The concept of a third force in the region paralleling the position of India, though disruptive to present tactical positions of the United States and Britain, would not necessarily prove disadvantageous to the long-run position of the West. A Maphilindo grouping would not be self-sufficient in either military or economic terms within the foreseeable future; the pattern of its component members' economies remains strongly oriented toward the West, and immediate dangers from internal subversion and external aggression stem mainly from the Chinese mainland. The United States and Britain, once they relinquished direct or indirect control over territories in the region, might find mutually profitable bases of association with the new complex, trusting to historic understandings achieved with the peoples of the Philippines and Malaya to curb the anti-Western outlook of the Indonesian regime. An assumption that any nascent Maphilindo would be dominated by Indonesia in its initial stages underestimates the ability of the Philippine Republic to serve as a countervailing force in terms both of economic strength and as a cultural focus for the loyalty of peoples of Malay origin. Of course, the position of the Philippines in any Malay grouping would depend to a considerable extent on the attitude adopted by the United States toward a neutralist Maphilindo—if favorable, the Philippines would be presented with leadership opportunities; if hostile, the Indonesian outlook might predominate. Evaluation in terms of Western interests of the success of a potential Maphilindo as against maintenance of a separate and excluded Malaysia depends on the importance placed on measures of direct control over areas that have achieved independent status; it was the retention of British and United States military bases in Singapore, Malaya, and the Philippines that was imperiled by Sukarno's threat "to crush Malaysia." The British "presence" in Malaysia evoked Indonesian hostility on the grounds that it presented a principal obstacle to association of the Malay states on a neutralist basis. To the Philippine government, a subtler objection to the British-inspired Federation of Malaysia was apparent—they considered British armed forces inadequate to deal with a gravely increased danger of subversion that followed its admission of leftist Chinese elements from Singapore and Sarawak to seats of power in Malayan politics. In the Philippine view, only the great centers of Malay population in Indonesia and their own country possess the strength to handle the problem of Chinese subversion throughout the region as a whole. Though the diplomatic reason for nonrecognition of Malaysia by the Philippine government was a claim to suzerainty over a portion of the former territory of North Borneo, the complicated legalism surrounding this demand made it clearly subject to international arbitration or settlement by the World Court should agreement be reached on the wider political questions involved. In contrast to Indonesia, the Philippines would lose rather than gain from any breakup of the integrity of Malayan states that would serve to augment the centripetal influence of their powerful neighbor. Accordingly, the Philippines appear well suited to represent a general Western interest in the formation of a viable and equal association of the peoples of Malay origin. In order that they may play this integrating role as Asians among Asians, the United States and Britain must enter into meaningful negotiations concerning the employment of military power centered on land bases within the territories of independent states constituting a potential Maphilindo confederation. The complete withdrawal of a physical presence appears unrealistic and probably harmful to the Malay nations themselves; there are, however, alternatives involving a use of military power to underwrite a general settlement in the Pacific area, acceptable to the security and advancement of the Maphilindo powers. The heart of the existing controversy with Indonesia, and to a lesser extent with the Philippines, is the claim of the United States and Britain to unilateral employment of force anywhere throughout the region, utilizing geographical bases of military power within the territories of states that are not consulted on policies that may result in disastrous reprisals on their peoples and lands. This attitude is becoming increasingly confined to the English-speaking states; it lacks support or even acceptance by France and such other European powers as may be attracted into the orbit of De Gaulle's statesmanship. When reduced to British, American, and French naked and conflicting national interests, the durability of the Western political position based on control of privileged bases of military strength appears uncertain in the face of a volcanic eruption of Asian nationalism with its concomitant manifestations of guerrilla strife.

As a consequence of the ruthless destruction of the communist apparatus in the slaughter of 1966, the relations of Indonesia to Malaysia and the Western powers in general have undergone a radical change. The personal commitments of Sukarno are no longer a decisive factor. Economic necessities dictate closer agreement with Western policies to offset the breach with Communist China. Underlying grievances against British and United States positions in Malaysia and elsewhere are, however, unlikely to be dissipated by immediate needs. Replacing the Sukarno policies of Indonesian aggrandizement under the guise of championing opposition to neocolonialism may require the creation of a new group of peninsular and insular powers as a third force in the organization of the Pacific peoples. Uncertainties clouding the foreign policy alignments of successor regimes to Sukarno in Indonesia hinder making predictions concerning the pace and character of future associations of the peoples of Malay origin. In May 1967, however, the Philippine and Indonesian Foreign Ministers agreed in principle to organize an economic-cultural-technical association, which would also include

Thailand, Malaysia, and Singapore. This new regional arrangement was declared supplementary to previous associations of more limited membership—that of the Association of Southeast Asia, consisting of Malaysia, the Philippines, and Thailand; and Maphilindo, consisting of Malaysia, the Philippines, and Indonesia.[9]

A wider perspective than has at present been manifested by the United States, Britain, and Australia will be required to influence this movement into channels favorable to Western interests. Some measure of equality of participation in Southeast Asian and Pacific affairs may have to be granted a grouping of nations that includes the Philippines, Indonesia, Malaysia, Singapore, and Thailand. Whether present strategic concerns permit the United States and Britain to make concessions that may involve partial abandonment of privileged military positions in the area of the Malacca straits, only immediate holders of executive power have the knowledge to decide and the authority to implement.

5 • THE POLICIES OF INDONESIA

The future course of Western interests in the Pacific realm will be determined to a considerable degree by political developments within the fifth most populous nation in the world, Indonesia, which is strategically located between the Pacific and Indian oceans. A series of crises, evoked in flamboyant emotional terms, have marred relations between Indonesia and the West since the close of the Japanese war. In each incident, attitudes within the Western complex have diverged, with no general agreement on a common policy toward Indonesian affairs. Thus, in its initial struggles to sever all ties with the Netherlands, the new republic received sympathetic support from Australia and the United States. In a pyrotechnic though bloodless campaign to include West Irian within her national boundaries, Indonesia retained the benevolent neutrality of the United States while encountering increasing opposition from Australia and the United Kingdom. Indonesia's next foray into the domain of a Western power—the "confrontation" of Malaysia—provoked the United Kingdom, Australia, and the United States into varying degrees of opposition but stimulated a measure of economic rapprochement with the Netherlands and perhaps her partners in the European Common Market.

President Sukarno's emotional diplomacy and erratic personality added to the impression of an immature nation indulging in irresponsible gestures without the inherent power or sense of direction to sustain a meaningful policy. This viewpoint may prove superficial, however, in the light of factors that are emerging in the total situation within the republic. In the perspective of its past history and present opportunities, certain attitudes may be presumed to have consolidated themselves into a basis for a foreign policy likely to be pursued by any Indonesian regime that has not degenerated into internal anarchy.

For example, Sukarno's doctrine of the "new emerging forces" as opposed to the "old established order" dramatized his country's ambition to assume leadership of the cultural and political evolution of offshore and peninsular Asia. Based on the nation's size, homogeneity, and independence, a valid argument can be made for Indonesian leadership of an aggregation of Pacific peoples, standing apart from both continental Asia and Western influence. Proselytizing nonalignment in this way is not necessarily hostile to the West, though it insists on a rigid differentiation of interests. Sukarno's assertion of Indonesia's claim to primacy in this region as the prophet of a "new order" paralleled the ambition of former President Nkrumah of Ghana to be regarded as the champion of Pan-Africanism. Sukarno has explained:

> The New Emerging Force is composed of the Asian nations, the African nations, the Latin American nations, the nations of the Socialist countries, the progressive groups in the capitalist countries . . . at least two thousand million people on the earth . . . the safety of the world is always threatened by the Old Established Order.[1]

Through the addition of a positive drive to the negative policy of nonalignment, Sukarno furthered regional autonomy. His theory of imperialism as a specific effort to subject all the peoples located on the route from the Atlantic Ocean to the Indian Ocean and the South China Sea introduced the concept of a "lifeline of imperialism" as a continuing factor in the tension between Western and Asian peoples. Sukarno postulated an inevitable conflict of interests based on the determination of Western powers to retain domination over major aspects of trade and economic development in the oceanic sphere. Neocolonialism, then, represented to him an active force requiring the combined resistance of all peoples formerly subject to colonial rule. Political independence, in his view, did not cure the situation if it was accompanied by continuing economic and military ties that retained a continuity of Western influence. For these reasons, Sukarno directed Indonesian external policy toward the objective of regional unity based on an aggressive autonomy.

Any effective Indonesian foreign policy must coincide with the realities of Indonesia's strategic location and the established bases of its economy and political pattern. Nationhood was won by the Indonesian people in the course of a struggle to free themselves from long-standing colonial rule. Both the nature of Netherlands domination and the process of winning independence have affected the character of the new nation. The arrogance of European colonialism as a historical episode manifested itself more openly in the East Indies than almost anywhere else in the world.

Western technology in the form of the far-faring sailing ship, equipped with firearms, resulted in the encounter of European and Eastern cultures during the sixteenth century. First Portugal and later Holland mounted a succession of armed trade raids against the Hindu, Buddhist, and Islamic states of Java and Sumatra. This intrusion has been compared, misleadingly, with previous impacts from India and the Arab world that assimilated the indigenous inhabitants to Hindu and Islamic culture groupings. A vital difference—one that affects present-day attitudes—lay in the European purpose to exploit resources for the profit of a distant homeland. Previous invaders may be regarded as religious and cultural missionaries who merged into the indigenous pattern of society.

As protagonists of Christianity or even Western technology throughout the East Indies, the Dutch must be accounted failures both in achievement and intent. Economic exploitation determined their policies of conquest and rule that held varying regard for human decencies and almost none for principles of cultural self-determination. The three and a half centuries of Netherlands domination were filled with almost continuous wars and rebellions—the Dutch conquest of the Sumatran state of Atjeh, for example, involved a devastating war that endured from 1873 to 1908. The pacification of the whole archipelago did not occur until the turn of the twentieth century, leaving only a few decades before the outbreak of the Japanese war for the Dutch to win the consensual loyalty of most of the Indonesian peoples to a Western association. Steps taken to bring the indigenous inhabitants into full participation in the control of their own affairs proved too little and too late to affect the situation. The profit motive still determined Dutch policy making; it has been estimated that by the 1930's 1 in every 7 of the 9 million residents of the Netherlands obtained an income directly or indirectly from the East Indies.[2] Though paternalistic Dutch management maintained decent standards of living among the inhabitants despite a rapid population increase, an artificial pattern was imposed on the country's economy to render it subservient to metropolitan interests. Education, technology, and industrialization were neglected in comparison with the advances being made in India or the Philippines.

Because of the unfavorable aspects of the colonial period, association with the West, even under conditions of political equality, has scant attraction for either the mass of the Indonesian community or their political elite. Economic illiteracy may prove only a surface explanation of the unwillingness of the present leadership to align their country with the course of industrial advancement predicated by commitment to the Western financial and trading system. The mass of the Indonesian people lack immediate experience of the beneficial workings of Western technology. According to a member of a United Nations Technical Mission:

> After 350 years of Dutch colonialism, the Indonesians had been drawn into the modern sector of the economy to an astonishingly small degree. In 1940 less than 10%

of the labor force was employed in that sector. Only about 5% of the Indonesian labor force was engaged in trade of any kind, and a still smaller percentage were small holders producing export products. At least 80% of the population still gained its livelihood in the traditional sector. Sumitro (Minister of Finance) has estimated that one half of one percent of the population (the Europeans) received 60% of the taxable national income, while the Chinese constituting another 2% of the population received 20% of the taxable national income. If these figures are correct, it would mean that Indonesians, constituting 97% of the population received only 20% of the taxable national income.[3]

The realities of the economic structure under which their supporters gain a livelihood condition political leadership into a skeptical approach to any Western connection. Sukarno's slogan of neocolonialism recognized the serious political obstacles facing any rapid transition into a pattern of technological culture along either Western or communist lines. Positive nonalignment is based on the incapacity to leap without further preparation from the long stasis that accompanied Dutch occupation into a fully industrialized society. With the possible exception of Burma, Indonesia was left by her colonial masters less adequately organized to direct her own economic development than any of her neighbors. India, the Philippines, and Malaya, though far from Westernized, possessed indigenous power groupings capable of directing the economy along Western lines. In the case of Indonesia, the link with the former economic system was almost severed through the forced departure of the 250,000 Dutch and Eurasian residents and later through the expulsion of many of the Chinese economic middlemen. The transition from colonialism has not ended with the grant of political independence; economic arrangements concerning rights of access by Western trade and industry to resources and markets within former colonies are under challenge. Because the Indonesian economy appeared to have the least to lose in terms of discontinuity, Sukarno's regime considered itself the natural leader in attempts to enforce a radical revision of the terms of economic relationship between Asian and Western cultures. From the point of view of long-range advancement of Western interests, it may prove realistic to accept Indonesia's position as the nucleus of a general resistance to the perpetuation of economic ties founded on assumptions conceived during the colonial era.

Indonesian nationalism, the emotional backbone of the political structure, has directed itself outward against former European rulers. The cultural homogeneity of the archipelago remains an objective rather than an established fact, as indicated by the national motto "Unity in Diversity." Regionalism kept the country in a condition of armed strife until 1962, conditioning the ordinary inhabitant to regard himself as Javan, Sumatran, or by some other traditional nomenclature, in preference to the recent Indonesian nationality. Indonesian political leadership was constrained to fan national unity along aggressive, anti-Western lines, with a glorification of guerrilla fighting against European forces as the symbol of national resolve. In consequence, no regime based on mass support would find it easy to reconcile partnership with any or all of the Western peoples with the slogans and attitudes that have come to be associated with concepts of independence. The dignified continuity that has characterized post-independence relations between the Philippines and the United States or the Commonwealth connection maintained by India and Malaya escaped the grasp of a people involved in active fighting against their former Dutch rulers. Independence, for Indonesian leadership, meant adoption of an aggressively regional attitude in international affairs. Suspicion of Western influence in any segment of the Pacific and Indian ocean regions may degenerate into open hostility under slight provocations. Thus an announced intention in 1963 to send units of the United States Seventh Fleet into the Indian Ocean resulted in mob action against the United States embassy at Jakarta and the statement by President Sukarno that "even if two, three, four or seven fleets want to deter Indonesia, we will continue to crush Malaysia." [4]

The political structure of the new republic affords some validity to Sukarno's thesis of a "new emerging force." At least, it is not readily identifiable in terms of Western institutional forms. Power loci do not appear to lie in political parties, social classes, bureaucratic organization, or an apparatus of dictatorship. In their place is a largely self-sufficient village structure of society, loosely molded into a political nation by centralized institutions of government that operate at low levels of professional skill and with a minimum of effective authority. Acceptance of the national idea, together with the absence of notable factional strains, appears to be the principal binding force. Disappearance of such feudal traits as marked rural organization in colonial days has removed from the political arena vital issues of land ownership and usage, touching on access to the means of production for most of the inhabitants. In consequence, government is not viewed by the village cultivator as primarily responsible for his economic condition; since he contributes little through taxation, his expectations of material benefits are overshadowed by the gain in personal dignity resulting from citizenship in a free nation. A regime able to sustain national enthusiasm, overcome regional divisions, and advance the importance of Indonesia in the outside world appears to satisfy many of the aspirations of its people. This consensual basis eliminates the need for authoritarianism, even under conditions of highly centralized control over national policy making.

The urban, trading, and industrialized segments of Indonesian society present different problems to the government structure. The virtual elimination of the European and Chinese class of merchants, owners, and administrators has, however, placed sufficient temporary patronage at the disposal of political rulers to ensure the immediate loyalty of the minority of educated and ambitious city dwellers. A government that is not under pressure to arbitrate bitter class or social divisions and is virtually supernumerary to the daily workings of the economy can afford to direct energies to the glamorization of the external relations of the nation. By Western standards, the reckless political handling of Indonesia's financial structure along with amateur economic planning would forfeit public confidence in the government responsible. Sukarno's regime, however, managed to breast the tide of chaotic inflation and obscured glaring mismanagement of the country's resources by the issuance of development plans based on a rhetoric of "democratic nationalism" and "Indonesian socialism." In practice, the economy, though stagnant in development and precarious in money terms, continued to sustain the bulk of the population in a manner to which they have become accustomed.

A true breakthrough into a modern industrialized society would, in all probability, require cooperation with outside investment on a scale that might be repugnant to the spirit of Indonesian nationalism. The decline of profitable trade between Indonesia and the rest of the world has been temporarily compensated by makeshift foreign aid that in turn has been largely sacrificed to further an aggressive foreign policy. In its Economic Survey for 1962, the United Nations Economic Commission for Asia and the Far East (ECAFE) stated that

> Indonesia developed an adverse balance of trade only after 1960, but its exports have made no sustained progress for many years. The main difficulties in regard to exports have been serious declines in the outputs of major crops and the disparity created by inflation and controls between domestic and foreign prices for export commodities. There was a further decline of 9 percent in export receipts during the first half of 1962. . . . Restrictions were so intensified as to cut imports by 14 percent. . . . Most types of consumer goods were heavily curtailed and the serious shortage of producer goods was further aggravated.[5]

Since 1963, export trade has been subordinated to political considerations arising from the confrontation of Malaysia and the consequent severing of ties with Singapore as an established channel of Indonesian trade.

Officially, government responsibility for the national economy is embodied in the 1960 National Over-All Development Plan (the Eight-Year Plan), compiled by Indonesian experts under the chairmanship of the late Professor Yamin. The ideological framework of this plan elaborates on the casual though revealing remarks of Sukarno in a

1959 speech: "The problem our country faces now is in the first place to provide our people with a good living. Therefore, the present is no time for too much theorizing. We had better be practical and pick out whatever is good from the ideas of Thomas Jefferson as well as those from Karl Marx—without, however, taking sides. In politics this is known as our active and independent policy." [6] Later rhetoric identifies Indonesian socialism as the "Mandate of the Peoples' Suffering," emphasizing its nationalist rather than internationalist preoccupations.

As a means of maintaining even a low level of economic association with the Western system, the plan presents an initial obstacle in its opposition to foreign capital investment. Loans and financial grants are envisaged as the external contribution to Indonesian development. But the technical basis for credit according to Western standards appears insecure; neither governmental tax plans nor domestic savings may be considered adequate to support the ambitious projects of the plan.[7]

Neither the existing strength nor future prospects of the Indonesian economy justify policies of military aggression directed against powerful neighbors. In this negative sense, then, the deteriorating economy ensures that Indonesia, despite political unfriendliness, will remain an unlikely source of military danger to Western interests. A bargaining position is still open both on the level of governmental aid and private investment to rescue Sukarno's or any succeeding regime from the pitfalls they may have dug for themselves through the pursuit of irresponsible policies. Previous contributions from the United States in the form of loans, outright grants, and favorable sales of agricultural surplus have been substantial. Between 1950 and 1962,

Indonesia obtained the equivalent of $710 million in American aid for civil purposes. From Soviet Russia approximately $1 billion was furnished for military equipment and around $650 million for nonmilitary purposes. Total foreign aid to Indonesia since independence has been estimated at around $3 billion,[8] and for most practical purposes the difference in value between what Indonesia was able to export and what she considered essential to import has been met from this source.

In consequence, the area of maneuver open to any Indonesian regime is limited by its dependent condition on the outside world. Thus, despite its severance of trade with Malaysia that reduced Indonesian exports by almost 50 percent and a general freezing of financial aid from Western sources, the Sukarno government secured approximately $250 million annually in foreign exchange by renegotiating contracts with three leading oil companies, two owned by American and one by British interests. A state visit to Moscow by President Sukarno in September, 1964, paid in political coin some of the obligations stemming from the billion dollar loan for military equipment. Communist China was mollified, notwithstanding the outbreak of anti-Chinese riots in Jakarta in 1963, by the hospitable reception given Liu-Shao-chi, titular Head of State of the People's Republic, which concluded with Sukarno and Liu cosigning a statement that "the two parties [Indonesia and Communist China] unanimously held that Imperialism and colonialism were the root causes of the threat to world peace and of international tension."[9] Subservience to any of the contending giants appears unlikely so long as benefits can be wrung from each of the separate camps.

The apparent formlessness of the Indonesian political

structure together with the peculiarity of its political processes creates a perhaps misleading impression of instability to Western eyes. Representative government founded on constitutional legality enjoyed brief tenure and its replacement in favor of consultative institutions avoided the customary forms of a one-party state or authoritarian dictatorship. The revolutionary constitution of 1945, reintroduced by decree in 1959, constituted the focal point of Sukarno's "guided democracy." This document was primarily an ideological declaration proclaiming the "Five Principles of Faith" in one god, humanity, nationalism, representative government, and social justice as the major objectives of political organization. Methods of achieving these ends were not translated by the original constitution into a framework of political institutions that would satisfy Western standards of workability and legalistic definition. A nostalgia for the communalistic traditions of Indonesian village life overshadowed borrowings from the machinery of Western representative government.

The sovereignty of the people was embodied in a People's Consultative Assembly serving as an electoral body for the choice of a president as well as a constitutional convention. This body was supposed to meet once in every five years and was to consist of members of Parliament and representatives of regions and functional groups. Its principal function was to select a president who was to become responsible to the nation only through this amorphous assembly. When the Sukarno regime abrogated a 1950 constitution, created by an earlier assembly, a Provisional People's Consultative Congress, with powers and composition similar to the former body, was appointed by the President himself. Parliament was downgraded from a representative institution, at least in Sukarno's phrase of "50 percent plus one democracy," and converted into an appointive body with primarily advisory powers. The name *gotong royong* Parliament given the new body signifies a concept, familiar on the village level, of voluntary effort for the common good. Executive and even legislative authority was concentrated under the President in a working Cabinet and in a Supreme Advisory Council of forty-five members, the latter body, however, meeting only five or six times a year. Final powers in the constitutional sense for both the initiation and the execution of policies rested with the President.

This consultative system under a strong leader was designed by Sukarno to incorporate age-old traditions of his people. Dealing with public affairs by processes of discussion leading to eventual unanimity under guidance of a venerated leader accords with the customs of centuries on the Indonesian village level. Though divergent from Western opinions concerning constitutional legality, the Sukarno system has parallels in the evolution of representative government in English-speaking lands. Stabilization of the nation-state in Tudor England followed a comparable conciliar pattern, directed by popular leadership under the then charismatic trappings of kingship. The tentative Indonesian attempt to reconcile traditions of ancient times with institutions of Western origin may not be dismissed as fantasies of a strong-minded eccentric.

Constitutional arrangements remain decorative paper work, of course, until they are brought into accordance with the realities of power groups. The Sukarno regime dispensed with the majority rule of a parliamentary system without creating a one-party state. Though a National Front organization, composed of representatives of numerous functional and political groups as well as regional and local branches, was constituted in 1960 under Sukarno's personal leadership, this body never achieved the position of a disciplined party monopolizing political and governmental power. Nor did the working machinery of state, bureaucratic, and police establishments develop into an effective weapon of social control available to the hands of a dictator. In practice, government authority remained a resultant of the tensions between well-balanced groups expressed through the person of the leader. As Sukarno described it to his audiences, ". . . I have explained hundreds and hundreds of times that revolutionary national *gotong royong* ways cannot possibly be effected without Nasakom at its hub—Nas-A-Kom (nationalist-religion-communist)—the three objective groupings into which the Indonesian People's political consciousness falls. . . ." [10]

The functioning of the Indonesian political process, then, was in part an adversary procedure with different elements of the community engaged in a fluctuating tug-of-war. Insofar as the state machinery, including the personality of the leader, remained uncommitted to any single group, policy direction could be controlled within the limits of a balance of contending forces. Nationalism was represented in effective power terms by the army, with the National Front far behind on the organizational level. An army mystique, based on its origin as a guerrilla force that spearheaded the struggle for freedom, served to identify the military with independence and national unity. This was furthered by the action of regional military commanders in maintaining the unitary concept of the nation against the "states' rights" rebellion fostered by traditional religionists. Conservative social elements regarded the armed forces as their principal protectors in the light of the army's role in crushing the communist rising of 1948 and its continuing hostility to the mass communist party of the Partai Kommunist Indonesia (PKI).

The economic and social basis of the army's power rests on two factors, its billion dollar financing in modern equipment by Soviet Russia and the control it exercised over the internal economic structure of the country through emergency regulations that were not lifted until 1963. In seeking to establish itself on an administrative level to counteract subversion, the army made unpopular moves that lessened its influence. The junior ranks of the military, however, enhanced community contact through roadbuilding and regional engineering works in partial imitation of the socially oriented United States Corps of Engineers.

On the other hand, the army lacks the kind of ideological cohesion that would make it a pliable instrument in the hands of a leadership group. A military take-over of the governmental apparatus is hindered by the loose organization of the officer corps and by a tendency toward autonomy on the part of the regional commanders. Between 1958 and 1961, a "colonels'" rebellion based in the outlying regions of Sumatra and Sulawesi split the armed forces without causing the higher command to desert the regime. Tolerant suppression of the revolt reinforced civilian supremacy over the military establishment as a whole.

Foreign policy decisions are, in part, conditioned by army needs and outlook. Indonesia's dependence on the Soviets to equip the armed forces on a scale that ensures superiority over its immediate neighbors, with the exception of mainland China, affects the political administration's freedom of maneuver in world affairs. Again, the army required the continuous presence of an "enemy" to justify its strength and the burden it imposed on the economy. When the Dutch finally relinquished the role of enemy with the cession of West Irian, it was more than a happenstance that Sukarno hastened to replace them with Malaysia and the British. Even the type of international opponent selected generally concurs with the army's predilections and capacities. Military involvements in the claim to West Irian and in the confrontation with Malaysia were both tailored to fit the army's taste for guerrilla warfare.

From the point of view of relations with the West, the army is a structural element that is likely to remain influential throughout possible shifts in policy or changes in the regime. Pressure for expansionist policies directed principally against territories of former colonial powers may be expected to be maintained as a justification of the army's strength—approximating 400,000 in 1964—and as a stimulant to the nationalist spirit that constitutes the army's esprit de corps. On the other hand, adventures in foreign policy involving open challenge to the sea and air power of the United States might encounter army opposition on professional grounds of disadvantage—guerrilla activities within contiguous areas provide the greatest opportunity for the successful exercise of Indonesian military strength. On the whole, the army appears to be a factor in Indonesian politics that is neither intrinsically hostile to Western interests nor favorable to current Western policies. It is conceivable that better integration of Western policy making, together with stricter regard for long-term interests, might result in designs for the region acceptable to the Indonesian armed forces.

Prior to October, 1965, the mass communist party of the

PKI constituted the second most powerful element in the pattern of Indonesian politics. An abortive attempt in 1948 to seize governmental power by force interrupted steady gains by communist leadership in the infiltration of the political and social structures. Later cooperation with the Sukarno regime was purchased at the price of comparative subordination of communist activities to Sukarno's non-ideological policies. Skillful use of the hostility between the army and the PKI permitted Sukarno to preserve the governing machinery of the bureaucracy as the instrument of his personal policies and of those of an educated class that was suspicious of communist discipline. The PKI steadily increased in numbers, however, to a membership of around 3 million, establishing a claim to be the largest communist party in the world outside communist-ruled countries. Its popular strength sufficed to limit policies in areas that might arouse its opposition. Thus the decision of the government to attempt financial and economic stabilization in 1962 with the help of Western funds was largely sabotaged by organized PKI action. The necessary domestic austerity program provided an opportunity for communist agitation to upset the political balance, influencing Sukarno to retreat into the distraction of the Malaysian confrontation.

Though unquestionably the leader, Sukarno did not appear an indispensable figure, nor was his focal position in the state based on any personal machinery of power. The Cabinet, though seldom called upon to make collective decisions, consisted of respected figures who discharged responsible ministerial functions as heads of major departments. A complex of dignified consultative bodies—the appointive Parliament, the National Planning Council, the

Supreme Council, and the executive body of the Interim People's Consultative Council—ensured that the President was at least well informed of the outlook of functional groups throughout the community.

The collapse of the precarious political balance achieved by Sukarno was occasioned by the "September 30th Movement" of 1965. A crudely conceived coup d'état, aimed at the elimination of the army hierarchy and its replacement by radical elements allied to the PKI, failed to gain its objective. The assassination of leading army officers provoked a countermovement directed against the PKI and its associates that proved beyond the power of Sukarno to control. In alliance with conservative Islamic elements, the educated and businessman middle class, and the ranks of the swollen bureaucracy, the army hierarchy overruled Sukarno's personal leadership. A massacre of PKI supporters, the full extent of which may never be determined, was perpetrated by Islamic factions with army support.

Despite the revolutionary character of the events, no substantial change was proclaimed in the official ideology of the republic. The continuity of the Indonesian revolution under the leadership of Sukarno, "Great Leader of the Revolution," was affirmed. In essence, the established hierarchy warded off a dangerous threat to its existence and employed the opportunity to win independence from the personal authority of President Sukarno. The task of stabilizing Indonesian nationhood, however, was similar to that faced by the Sukarno regime. Cultural and linguistic differences stand in the way of the island peoples' social unity. Where there is no widely used national language,[11] a national image has to be projected through charismatic personalities and readily understood slogans.

A cleavage between the economic needs of the city dwellers and the more self-sufficient countryside hampers concerted action to raise living standards. Formulas for economic growth based on Western concepts require major adaptation when applied to the Indonesian environment. On the other hand, a radical solution along Chinese Communist lines has been averted through the destruction of the communist PKI apparatus. The continuance of the Indonesian nation-state as an exemplar of "unity through diversity" appears highly probable, though the constitutional structure and political machinery to implement its development has not yet been clearly manifested.

From the point of view of Western interests, the most significant change is that affecting Indonesia's relations with neighboring lands. Sukarno's personal policy to win leadership for Indonesia in a "third world force" centered around Asian-African opposition to neocolonialism appeared in a state of collapse before the "September 30th Movement." A petulant swing into the orbit of Communist China aggravated domestic tensions and hastened the downfall of the President's personal authority. The confrontation with Malaysia degenerated into a military fiasco that embarrassed the army, and any popular enthusiasm it aroused was not enough to offset the serious injury it inflicted on the Indonesian economy. Sukarno's ill-conceived withdrawal of Indonesia from the United Nations was accorded the ignominy of international indifference. Indeed, it was so carelessly executed that both the succeeding Indonesian administration and the United Nations Secretariat have been able to argue that it was never officially consummated and that Indonesia could resume her seat without formal readmission.

Whatever final disposition is made of Sukarno and his foreign policies, succeeding regimes face similar incentives to engage Indonesia fully in world politics. The assertion of Indonesian leadership over a group of Pacific peoples rests on its position as the largest nation of Malay origin. The need for Indonesian internal cohesion requires popular identification with expansionist policies based on cultural similarities. If enthusiasm for a destiny associated with wider cultural ties should falter, the Indonesian revolution may be wrecked on the shoals of jealous provincialism. A nationalist Indonesian government is bound to direct its external relations toward collaboration with the Philippines, Malaysia, and other Pacific peoples of Malay stock, either through amicable agreement or forced association.

Stabilization of an Indonesian regime around a hieratic structure of military and civilian bureaucracy may intensify activity in external affairs. An army must maintain a popular image, in relation to its size, power, and cost to the community, as a body essential to national defense and expansion. If no external enterprises demand a display of military might, the armed forces assume a police guise that arouses more popular hostility than support. The civilian bureaucracy for its part draws much of its authority from the needs of advancing technology. In the existing circumstances of Indonesia, the growth of industrialization depends on the establishment of profitable relations with advanced industrialized communities in the rest of the world. The United States, Europe, Japan, the Soviet Union, and Communist China provide Indonesian statesmen with a variety of choices from which to construct an economic foreign policy. During the period in which this choice is being determined, Western interests are presented with the opportunity to influence the course of Indonesian policies in their favor. It is, however, an opportunity shared with international rivals.

The present disadvantage of the Western group lies in a shortsighted disunity that makes a common policy in Pacific affairs unattainable by the statesmen of the United States, Britain, France, and Australia. There is even question as to whether Japan should be included in the Western system or relegated to a subordinate or competing position. Uncertainty as to the nature or even existence of their own collective interests handicaps the Western powers in their evaluation of the basic drives likely to govern Indonesian foreign policy. It may be ventured that the strictly nationalist policies of individual Western powers are unlikely to find support from any Indonesian government. So long as each Western nation persists in a unilateral pursuit of economic and military advantage in the Pacific area, Indonesian interests will run counter to those of the West. The anticolonialism that sparked the Indonesian revolution is now directed against military power used unilaterally to influence the destinies of overseas peoples. Though the accusation of neocolonialism is primarily emotional, some substance for the charge may be found in the control exercised over the Pacific basin as a communications center and base for military operations by a loose confederation of non-Asian powers.

6 • FRANCE
IN THE PACIFIC

The economic and political stability achieved by the Fifth Republic within metropolitan France has permitted the revival of a French thesis on future relations between the peoples of Europe and the Far East. Though De Gaulle's outstanding prestige has personalized this thesis, it amounts in fact to a reaffirmation of historic French attitudes toward relations between technologically advanced cultures and emergent ones. In the rhetoric of a former French Minister of Colonies:

> France has been colonizing, in the noblest sense of the term, for the last thousand years. In the words of one of our historians, she has always sought to spread outward—from her natural desire to know people and the world, to expand, found and create. For more than a thousand years she has radiated in the direction of Asia;

the ancient Gauls over-ran Greece, the Normans conquered Sicily, the French Crusaders conquered the Holy
Land.[1]

This enlargement of French culture, conceived of as a
mission civilisatrice, is based on concepts that are practical
in their import though foreign to Anglo-Saxon patterns of
thinking. A legacy from the French Revolution is a moti-
vating belief in human fraternity and the solidarity of all
mankind as a corrective to selfish nationalism. Though in
practice this world outlook was corrupted almost at once
through techniques of military conquest and forced assimilation of weaker peoples, a supranational concept of cultural exchange remained a tenet of the French national
conscience. The diminution of her relative power position
has refined much of the imperialistic flavor from French
attitudes toward emergent peoples; for the time being at
least, the spread of French civilization takes precedence
over power advantages to the French state. This is expressed
in practice by the priority given efforts to relieve the pau-
perism indigenous to Africa and Asia, an enterprise to
which the French people have committed themselves more
fully, proportionate to their national income, than any other
Western state.

The idealism that distinguishes French sympathy toward
underdeveloped peoples is based on an assessment of the
shifting importance of influence as against power in achieving world leadership. A preoccupation with recently acquired military supremacy has, perhaps, clouded American
perception of the significance of technological and cultural
exchanges in providing leadership advantages to well-
equipped national communities. There is little contradiction
between intense French nationalism and their willingness

to contribute French technology and culture to the advancement of other peoples without insisting on ideological conformity or political concessions. Though a shrewd gamble on developing capacities of insurgency to offset conventional military forces may underlie immediate French tactics, the long-term principle involved envisages technological superiority as preferable to political control in establishing advantageous relations with a majority of the world's peoples. A degree of skepticism toward the type of international justice obtainable through organs such as the United Nations also distinguishes French policy from that of its Atlantic associates; a pluralism of cultural influences competing as foci for less-advanced communities attracts French policy makers as a more logical development for a world in which technology rather than politics promises to become the unifying influence. Translated into terms of current policy in the Far East, the French thesis may be described as one of nonintervention in both the practices and ideologies of indigenous politics in favor of maximum stimulation along cultural and technological lines.

Among the Pacific islands, France, through the clarity of her policy toward indigenous peoples, which accepts them as French citizens participating in the culture and economy of the motherland, has established for herself a unique position in relation to other colonizing powers. Neither the size, strategic location, nor the economy of French Polynesia and New Caledonia are of sufficient consequence for them to be accounted of major importance in Pacific affairs. However, on the level of Western dealings with peoples of Melanesian, Micronesian, and Polynesian origin, France, by acknowledging the right of people at their cultural level to full acceptance in a Western state, has seized an initiative that may prove difficult to overcome. Regional plans designed by Britain, Australia, and the United States for their preponderant holdings in this area will, from now on, be conditioned by the political and cultural status of French Polynesians—if equal citizenship on the French model is withheld, can physical possession be maintained on naked grounds of strategic need?

New Caledonia, a major exporter of nickel and the world's third largest producer of chrome, is the French Pacific territory of most direct concern to Americans, who not only import the bulk of its chrome production but have now replaced British capital as principal investor in this mining interest. The comparatively large land surface of New Caledonia (8,548 square miles) is rich in minerals, with nickel and chrome predominating over less valuable deposits of manganese and iron ore. From its geographical position, approximately on the Tropic of Capricorn some 500 miles northeast of Brisbane, the economy of the island would appear naturally linked to neighboring Australia, where essential imports can be obtained at considerably less cost than those borne on the long voyage from Europe or the United States. France's economic dominance is assured, however, because Australian consumption of chrome is insufficient to balance trade relations if Australian imports to New Caledonia were substantially increased.

The stratification of the population adds an unusual factor under South Seas conditions—in 1960, the inhabitants were estimated as 78,000, of which 38,500 were Melanesian *Canaques,* 27,000 were Europeans, some were of mixed breeding, and a fluctuating number of Asians had been reduced by repatriation to around 12,000. Labor for the mining industry, formerly indentured from Tonkin (now North Vietnam) and Indonesia, is now drawn from well-paid European technicians who operate highly mechanized processes. Emigrants from Italy and elsewhere contribute to this skilled force that has raised the number of residents of European origin in the capital at Nouméa to 11,000 out of a total urban population of 18,000. On the other hand, the tribal *Canaques* have had an unhappy history, probably on account of the original use of the territory as a penal settlement. Driven from their traditional homes in the hill areas, more by ravages of imported cattle than through the annexation of their lands, they engaged in a savage revolt in 1878, massacring more than 200 Europeans and gourmandizing on many of their victims. The persistence of cannibalism, which had degenerated from a religious rite into a dietary addiction, created barriers between European settlers and the indigenous people until comparatively recent times. Rule over village life has been substantially relegated to customary chiefs, though their authority is now undermined by a general acceptance of Christianity and the introduction of a money economy. Subsistence agriculture with some dependence on coffee as a cash crop constitutes the economic basis of indigenous life—comparatively low standards for Melanesian society may be deduced from 1951 figures that show a death rate of 20 percent for *Canaques* as compared with 8 percent for the European element. Social contact between tribal villagers and the European residents lags well behind political concepts of equal citizenship, for obvious cultural reasons unconnected with race prejudice. The technical standards stimulated by the mining industry together with a high degree of economic prosperity among Europeans have reduced the practicability of assimilation comparable to that prevalent in Tahiti. Indigenous problems in island politics —reversion to primitive religious practices and hostility toward the influence of missionaries—bestow an air of unreality to claims of identification with metropolitan France, and they open the door to subversion from Asian quarters.

The immediate political situation, however, is concerned with internal divisions among the European group—the permanent residents' distrust of transient administrative personnel from the home government and economic rivalry between the more numerous class of *petits colons,* small ranchers and store keepers, and the power holders in the larger corporate interests controlling the economy. The agricultural base of the economy, above the level of subsistence cultivation, appears poorly organized and generally retrograde. Continuous erosion of tropical soil, naturally phosphate-poor, combined with an overly dry climate operates against a plantation economy, that is weakened in any case by a labor shortage aggravated by the withdrawal of indentured Asian workers and the continuing inability to recruit indigenous villagers. A complicating factor is the uneconomic size, under tropical conditions, of the properties of the majority of planters. Thus, in the 1950's, European ranchers were viewed as falling into three categories: *petits colons,* numbering 1,000, with average holdings of 10 hectares, cultivated only 3 percent of the total land owned by Europeans; *colons éleveurs,* about 800 in number, farmed 25 percent of the area in holdings that averaged 100 hectares; and, finally, the remaining 72 percent of the plantation land was in the possession of 100 *grands éleveurs* or corporations operating average areas of 2,000 hectares. The social conflicts between these groups, aggravated by the provincialism of an isolated, insular community, hinder the grand designs of the metropolitan government for a showplace of French culture and national integrity in the heart of an Anglo-Saxon sphere of influence.

Nevertheless, the Fifth Republic's achievements in imposing French leadership over future developments in the Pacific realm remain notable even within the limited framework provided by New Caledonia and its minor dependencies, the Loyalty Islands and the Island of Pines; all inhabitants are now French citizens enjoying universal suffrage, which they employed to affirm their status as an overseas territory of France by a 96 percent majority in the referendum of 1958. On the national scene, the territory of New Caledonia is represented in the Parliament of Paris by one deputy and a single senator. A popularly elected Territorial Assembly of thirty members possesses consultative authority over island affairs and considerable powers over the budget. The High Commissioner, however, as the representative of the Republic, retains a veto power over the assembly's deliberations as well as supreme executive power. Since 1956, in accordance with the *loi-cadre* of that year applicable to all French territories overseas, a Government Council, presided over by the High Commissioner, has had the authority to promulgate by-laws and prepare a budget for submission to the assembly. Though this council of seven ministers elected by the assembly represents a mild dilution of the authority of the Paris-appointed High Commissioner, the colonial-type "Governor" is still the mainspring of official action, preserving a long-established cleavage between the bureaucracy in Paris and the outlook of the island residents.

Apart from the obvious inability of the small group of Europeans to defend themselves as a separate political entity, the need for the French connection is illustrated by the financial and technical aid contributed by the metropolis. A 1960 export value of $50.6 million balanced against imports of $37.8 million would appear to make the territory self-sufficient; nevertheless, the metropolitan Fonds d'Investissement et Développement Economique et Sociale (FIDES) have contributed intelligently to the growth of prosperity. Thus an urgent need to process nickel ore to save transportation costs is being met by the construction of a hydroelectric project, which is financed in part by FIDES. Between 1946 and 1960, FIDES expended $14.2 million in New Caledonia, of which $6.6 million were earmarked for social equipment. As a consequence, the transition of the indigenous majority toward a technological culture has been accelerated; 96 percent of school age children attend school; a technical vocational school at Nouméa has 300 students; and more advanced students, both European and assimilated natives, are brought up to the level of the French baccalauréat at the Collège La Pérouse. Perhaps even more significant is the work of the Institut Français d'Océanie, an active research center in agricultural, medical, oceanographic, geophysical, biological, and ethnological sciences that not only contributes to the fundamental development of the French Pacific territories but also serves as a resource center for the international South Pacific Commission, whose headquarters are located at Nouméa. The technical and intellectual leadership accorded Nouméa through possession of outstanding facilities constitutes an important factor in France's claim to make her voice heard in determining general policies for the Pacific realm.

New Hebrides, under a condominium government of

French and British composition, exemplifies to the point of absurdity the ill effects of archaic European rivalries on the well-being and development of Pacific islanders. Situated northeast of New Caledonia, the New Hebrides group of islands covers a land area of 5,700 square miles and is inhabited by some 60,000 Melanesians, who are akin to the Solomon islanders. During the chaotic scramble for dominion in the latter half of the nineteenth century, neither the French nor the British established clear political supremacy, though French residents and interests came to predominate. As part of the *Entente Cordiale* that preceded World War I, a protocol for the New Hebrides was framed in 1914 establishing a condominium government; at the close of that war, France's request for undivided possession was denied by Britain at the instigation of Australia. United Kingdom concern in the area never amounted to more than a cloak for the protection of Australian commercial and strategic interests. In 1961, the protocol was emended by an exchange of notes between the two participating governments that did little more than alter administrative details.

France's claim to control the destiny of the islands rests on the fact that cultivated plantations in French hands are over ten times greater in area than corresponding British holdings; also, residents of French origin make up two-thirds of the total European population of 2,000. The British-Australian interest is based on a preservation of trade privileges; though Australia enjoys a $3 million business in annual imports into the New Hebrides, she accepts barely one-fifth of the islands' exports; most of the copra, the main product of the area, is shipped a costly route to France. Behind the attitudes of the metropolitan governments may be discerned rivalries of two of the great corporate shipping and trading concerns that have long exercised semisovereign power in Pacific regions, the Australian firm of Burns Philp and the French company *Messageries Maritimes*.

European intervention has achieved little for the betterment of the indigenous inhabitants. It has maintained the economy of the island on the level of a copra plantation—credit for such advances as have been made in the production of cocoa and coffee may be attributed almost entirely to French planters. Following the cessation of the forced recruitment of Melanesians and indentured workers from Indochina, labor requirements for plantation cultivation have become a major problem. Some Asians, however, who rejected repatriation at the close of their indentured service now constitute mobile work forces that move from plantation to plantation and operate with considerable independence and efficiency. Compared with those in corresponding regions under the direct colonial rule of either Britain or France, the efforts made to improve health or education within the Melanesian community must be considered ridiculous. The political status of the indigenous peoples is equally amorphous—neither Britain nor France permits its colleague-rival to apply its national concepts for the political advancement of the inhabitants. Since 1961, a token concession to the indigenous Melanesians has increased their membership on the consultative council to the resident administrators from one-third to one-half. A three-year economic development plan for a capital investment of $1,711,920 on roads, communications, agricultural improvements, and other projects was launched by the joint rulers in 1966. An increased assimilation of indigenes into higher administrative ranks is also reported. The wasteful division of schools into French and British systems continues, however, with the prospect of one French and one English school on a secondary level opening in 1966 to provide education to the islanders above the secondary level for the first time.

The consequences of the current dog-in-the-manger attitude that isolates the New Hebrides from the mainstream of political and social advance in the South Seas may seem negligible against the background of world politics; copra islands barely out of stone-age culture appear to call for little attention from harassed statesmen. Significant issues of Western security, however, are impinged upon by the existing situation. In the first place, the consensus of European and North American nations required to implement common policies for the future of Pacific peoples is endangered through manifestations of petty rivalries between France and Australia centered on the New Hebrides condominium. A suspicion, prevalent in France and other European countries, that the Anglo-Saxons used their Pacific victory to oust their lesser allies from previous spheres of influence is sustained by an unrealistic clinging to historic claims that is an obvious obstacle to progress. The tortoise-like advance toward common Western action in the Pacific realm provided by the South Pacific Commission is subject to, and has been subjected to, a French veto. Evidence of the good faith of her Anglo-Saxon associates will have to be forthcoming before the France of De Gaulle, or any other likely regime, will open the Pacific for joint action by the Western peoples. The discontent and open resistance of New Hebrides Melanesians may be of minor account (in the face of their total lack of arms), except where it may provide an opportunity for outside intervention. This may come from the United Nations General Assembly Committee on the Situation with Regard to the Implementation of the Declaration of Independence to Colonial Countries and Peoples—the so-called Committee of Seventeen, established in 1961 and largely dominated since then by Asian and African members. The situation could provide a convenient whipping post for Western "imperialism." Of graver concern, it could give an excuse to Indonesian expansionism to champion the cause of the residue of Asian workers, merge it with that of the indigenous peoples, and intervene as the natural liberator against the rule of a divided European minority.

A political situation in the French protectorate of Wallis and Futuna parallels the British relationship to the Kingdom of Tonga. This small archipelago northeast of Fiji is peopled by about 9,000 Polynesian kinsfolk of the Tongans and is undisturbed by European planters or Asian contract labor. Though in a 1959 referendum the inhabitants chose the status of an overseas territory of France, the logic of assimilation or association has been largely disregarded to permit continuity of indigenous customary rule. France's role is that of external protector, and she exploits island resources only to the extent of directing more adventurous workers to the labor markets of New Caledonia or New Hebrides. A nostalgic flavor of anthropological romance finds expression in the comment of a contemporary French authority: "This little world in miniature, very isolated, inhabited by an amiable, lazy people untroubled by contact with Europeans, is certainly one of the more original existing in the isles of the Pacific." [2]

The core of French colonialism in the Pacific realm is

centered in the overseas territory of French Polynesia, formerly known as Les Établissements Français de l'Océanie, a group of five archipelagos: the Society Islands, the Gambier Islands, the Marquesas Islands, the Taumotu Archipelago, and the Austral Islands. From any commercial or strategic point of view, these small volcanic or coral islands that extend over 1,550 miles of latitude in the tropical zone and are located over 4,000 miles from San Francisco and less than 2,000 miles from Sydney are of minor significance. Tahiti in the Society group overshadows all the other islands as the home of more than half the 80,000 population of French Polynesia; Papeete, its capital, boasts more than 16,000 residents. Land usage, based on an economy of coconuts, vanilla, and coffee growing, is almost wholly in the hands of indigenous inhabitants; phosphate deposits in the Taumotu Archipelago contribute to an export trade that failed, however, to balance imports by more than $5 million in 1960. Population growth and rising living standards create strains on the island's resources, but these strains have been offset since the close of the Japanese war by contributions from the metropolitan government—between 1946–1960 funds advanced by FIDES amounted to $13,360,300.

It is in the political sphere that events in French Polynesia possess significance for the Western world in general, particularly since it provides a testing ground for the French thesis of decolonization as contrasted with Anglo-Saxon practice. In the logic of French history, contacts with less-developed peoples progress through a period of tutelage and partial cultural assimilation to various degrees and forms of association. Though political independence is now accepted as an inevitable development in major areas, it is not equated with any final breach in the continuity of association. Accordingly, the spread of French cultural and economic influence among underdeveloped peoples is a major objective of the Fifth Republic, a policy backed by expenditure from metropolitan funds of approximately $2 billion annually, or around 2.4 percent of France's gross national product. This may be contrasted with United States expenditures of $4.2 billion for this purpose, equivalent to only 0.7 percent of the gross national product.[3] In light of this dedication, France is averse to internationalization of the liquidation of colonial empires, either through the machinery of the United Nations or other means. In the Pacific realm, France offers a clear opportunity to peoples under her control to engage in the development of their isolated regions as part of a cultural and economic complex where they enjoy the dignity and privileges of citizens of France in addition to the technical and financial support that such an advanced European state can offer her outlying territories. Neither Britain, the United States, nor Australia offers its wards equivalent terms for continued association, for they apparently assume that Western culture is at present beyond the practical reach of Pacific peoples. An Anglo-Saxon view that French cultural and political expansionism is a romantic illusion bereft of the realities of effective force or historic logic merits closer examination; at its least, the French thesis presents a problem to be resolved before any joint action for furtherance of Western interests in the region may be attempted and, at its best, it may pioneer alternative solutions to the contradictions of existing Anglo-Saxon policies.

Tahiti, then, as a unique political phenomenon in the Pacific presents in miniature many of the difficulties and opportunities inherent in continuing relations between Pacific and Western peoples. From an American viewpoint, significant parallels exist between the situation in Tahiti and conditions in the Commonwealth of Puerto Rico or in the Virgin Islands; in both cases, the pressure of population growth against environmental resources necessitates drastic changes in life and the economy to ensure adequate living standards and employment for the fast-swelling work forces. This basic economic problem spurs the transition of static, provincial cultures into the mainstream of metropolitan technology, but it creates social tensions of identity, loyalties, and acceptance. The political structure has to bear the burden of unavoidable social confusion by providing new incentives for the individual and fresh sources of authority for the ordering of the general society. Puerto Rico and the Virgin Islands, in outstripping other island groups in the Caribbean area in adapting their economies and culture to technological standards, have rooted their accomplishments in forms of political association with a major Western power. It is the particular form of union that is significant; the mere fact of association can have different and less noteworthy results, as exemplified by the former British West Indies. Citizenship for its people in the American union, with all the legal and moral responsibilities that arise in mainland institutions, triggered the transformation of Puerto Rico; though complex political and social problems resulted, and remain imperfectly resolved, a major contribution to the betterment of a deprived segment of the world's peoples was unquestionably achieved. On a minor scale a similar pattern is being attempted in Tahiti.

French citizenship, accompanied by universal suffrage and representation in the metropolitan Parliament, was accorded the Polynesian inhabitants of Tahiti in 1945; in the brief decades following, a political structure along Western lines of party politics has emerged, without as yet crystallizing into stable form. Politics, revolving around the principal question of relations with metropolitan France, has, however, become a major factor in determining the direction of economic and social progress; it bypasses ethnic and occupational divisions to create a common purpose. Though 87 percent of the inhabitants are of prevalently Maori origin, the mores of tribal life are largely superseded by a general European system of education and active membership in village Protestant churches; a distinctive peasant outlook, however, protects the homogeneity of the rural areas against the more volatile, urban attitudes of Papeete. Residents of European or Chinese origin feel sufficiently free of racial concerns to choose political affiliations based on occupational and personal considerations relating to taxes, labor relations, and the degree of control that may be legitimately exercised by transient metropolitan officials.

As an integral part of France, Tahiti ratified De Gaulle's constitution for the Fifth Republic by a 63.7 percent majority of the electorate. Subsequently, the Territorial Assembly reaffirmed the status of French Polynesia as an overseas territory with a constitutional structure composed of a popularly elected Assembly, a Council of Government elected by the Assembly, and a Governor appointed from Paris. Members of the Council of Government exercise individual ministerial functions as heads of departments. In the style of the Fifth Republic, the governor, as the final repository of executive authority, retains reserve powers over the conduct of departments as well as supervision over legislative actions. Control over the budget is divided between the Assembly and the Governor by the device of obligatory and optional sections; the former, dealing with essential expenditures for official salaries and the maintenance of public order, may be decreed by the Governor should the legislature prove obdurate. The position of the Governor as representative of the metropolis is a source of underlying tensions between his office and the locally elected Assembly. A Permanent Commission of the Assembly, composed of five members, exercises delegated power between sessions and streamlines the legislative function to suit the needs of a small and dispersed community. As in France, the governmental system is weighted in favor of centralization, with minor powers accorded local district organization. The homogeneous bulk of Polynesian voters, however, resides in rural districts, and its political strength in the central assembly offsets the administrative subordination of localities.

Establishment of party politics as a means of resolving social and economic tensions provides a crucial test of the affiliation of French Polynesia to a Western social order; adoption of communal politics or a dictatorial regime would tend to draw the inhabitants into the orbit of major protagonists on the Asian mainland. Two main issues appear to have emerged in the early stages of party politics in Tahiti. One is the nature of relations with France, and it ranges from demands for full independence to cultural and political identification. The other issue is the relative power position of the Polynesian peasant and worker majority as against the economic superiority of an urban group in Papeete. Though ethnic and communal rivalries are downgraded by virtue of civilized French attitudes toward racial admixtures, social divisions are based on wide divergencies of cultural traditions and economic outlooks. In the early 1950's, the situation was dramatized by the rise of Pouvanaa a Oopa, a demagogue who attracted support from the peasant countryside and certain elements within the urban trade unions. Combining some of the attributes of messianic cargo cults with Protestant sectarianism and radical labor policies, Pouvanaa retained a personal following of approximately 70 percent of the electorate from his initial election as Tahitian representative in the French Parliament in 1949 until his conviction in 1958 on the charge of conspiracy to burn down public buildings in Papeete. Whether or not Pouvanaa and his consistently victorious party, the Rassemblement Démocratique des Populations Tahitiennes (RDPT), represented a genuinely national movement that aimed at separation from France has been a question of vital concern to the future of the territory. Professor Guiart, a contemporary authority on France in the Pacific, is of the opinion that the RDPT was never a true secessionist movement, and Senator Coppenrath, the Tahitian member of the French Senate, points out that, when Pouvanaa himself advocated independence in the referendum of 1958, 64 percent of the electorate voted to remain with France.[4] Since the downfall of Pouvanaa as leader, the RDPT has become factionalized, and a united opposition party of more conservative hue, the Union Tahitienne Démocratique (UDT), succeeded to power. The failure of Pouvanaa's charismatic leadership to overturn established economic and social bonds may be largely attributed to the real power centers of village life—the Protestant congregations—who repudiated his movement when he became a threat to the essential unity of the territory.

A new element has been introduced into Tahiti's relation to the Western world through De Gaulle's insistence on conducting nuclear test explosions on the coral reefs of Fangataufa and Mururoa, several hundred miles from Papeete. Despite the protest of the Tahitian Deputy to the French National Assembly, the danger of pollution remains minor. The feelings of Tahitians about this involvement, however, is likely to be more critical and sophisticated than the corresponding reaction of the inhabitants of the American-controlled Marshall Islands. Another disturbing factor may center around the intrusion of a scientific and military community concerned with the apparatus of testing. The delicate balance between residents both indigenous and ethnically French and transient metropolitans is likely to be further imperiled. It seems possible to claim that sufficient unity of social and economic interests in the island chain has been achieved to permit progress through orderly, democratic processes, thus linking Tahiti to the culture system of France and the West in general. To forecast future evolution parallel to that of Hawaii might be rash in view of the small proportion of European residents, the great distances involved in contacts with the metropolis, and the paucity of economic resources. It would appear reasonable, however, for the United States, Britain, and Australia to consider France's experiment in Polynesia a pilot test of the adaptability of South Seas peoples and to render it befitting support.

7 • THE PLACE OF THE ANTIPODEAN NATIONS: AUSTRALIA AND NEW ZEALAND

The immediate future may witness a sharp rise in the significance of "residential" qualifications as against "absentee landlordism" in the determination of policies for the Pacific realm. The era of naked power probably ended with the defeat of imperial Japan; subsequent American force has filled a temporary vacuum without pretending to create a system of its own. In postwar times, the lands of the Pacific have been subjected to a competition of systems infiltrating their economic, social, and ideological foundations—an impact from the outside world increasingly conditioned by factors other than military or economic power.

Western influence, diffused through centuries of colonial dominance, no longer rests on the might of metropolitan powers in Europe and North America; in place of a supremacy based on force, institutional patterns derived from the West face pragmatic tests as to their applicability to regional needs and ideals. The advancement of Western values, as contrasted with those advocated from the Asian land mass, necessitates participation in regional affairs to a point of total commitment. Logically, such involvement depends on geographical propinquity; Australia and New Zealand, for example, are Pacific countries by location and Western only by tradition. In their case, the future of the Pacific realm embraces their only possible destiny, rendering them the most directly engaged champions of a Western point of view.

There are two possible explanations as to why the antipodean nations have not been entrusted with a higher degree of leadership of Western influence in the Pacific realm; in the first instance, residual nationalism may dictate power policies that pay only lip service to any overriding conflict of world systems. Second, Australia and New Zealand may be accounted imperfect champions of the West in terms of their cultural organization and their power to influence their geographical regions. Both reasons have been in evidence since before the Japanese war, and the degree of their justification rests with historians of international affairs. Growing regional tensions, based on color, ideologies, and power shifts, have thrust interrelationships between the antipodean nations and their Western counterparts into the forefront of political attention. In simple terms, is the West united behind a guarantee of the territorial integrity of the Commonwealth of Australia as an indivisible extension of Western culture in the Pacific? If so, does such a guarantee commit Western powers, particularly the United States, to the prevailing domestic policy of a "White Australia," sustained by immigration bars directed against a possible admixture of peoples? Are the Western nations, specifically the United States, Britain, and France, prepared to center regional organization of South Seas peoples under their present control around an antipodean heartland of Western culture and technology in preference to preserving them as dependents of geographically remote metropolitan governments? In the light of the defense actualities of the region, what terms of co-operation and acceptance of common Western policies, even those impinging on domestic affairs, will be expected of the peoples of Australia and New Zealand by their American protectors? Even raising questions of this character for consideration may exacerbate relations between the United States and Australia, hitherto noteworthy for an ease largely based on avoidance of awkward issues. However, the stirring nations of the Orient and the political awakening of the island peoples of the Pacific present problems that they are unlikely to submit to the amateur balm of "gentlemen's agreements." Though the rampant claims of Indonesia as a non-Western organizer of the Pacific area may fizzle out in the bankruptcy of its power and leadership, they serve as a portent of storms capable of being unleashed by Asian powers. The place of the antipodean nations in an inevitable struggle for the survival of a Western presence in Asia and the Pacific requires a realistic appraisal to avoid entrapment in conflicts alien to the true interests of Western civilization.

The degree of formal partnership existing between Australia, the United States, and Britain in the Pacific is difficult to determine in the light of the changing flux of Asian affairs. What at the outset was viewed as a limited guarantee of the territorial integrity of Australia and New Zealand against further aggression on the part of Japan has apparently involved the United States in contingent liability for the defense of Australian territory, wherever situated, from any external menace. As part of the price paid by John Foster Dulles for Australian acceptance of the unilaterally negotiated treaty with Japan, the United States concluded a defense treaty with Australia and New Zealand. This tripartite arrangement of 1951 (ANZUS), from which Britain was purposefully excluded, did not initially contemplate common defense arrangements extending over the whole area of the Pacific, nor, in fact, was any future enemy other than Japan—or more remotely Red China—envisaged. A decade later, Indonesia's eruption into the power politics of the area through its occupation of West Irian and its challenge to Malaysia provoked a statement that the United States would support Australian defense of New Guinea and Papua against attacks from any quarter.[1] Whether this was a special case or whether a commitment may now be assumed for the mutual defense of all Pacific possessions by the ANZUS powers remains obscure. The collective defense of the whole Southeast Asia region through an alliance of the independent nations of the area with major Western powers proved unattainable; failure of Asian countries beyond Thailand, Pakistan, and the Philippines to become signatories reduced the significance of the Southeast Asia Treaty Organization (SEATO) from its inception. Its present status, as discussed in a following chapter, may be described as a focus for diplomatic confusion. In consequence, the more concrete realities of the ANZUS agreement have increased in scope and importance as illustrated by a communiqué is-

sued at the close of the June, 1963, meeting of the alliance
to the effect that "a threat to any of the partners in the
Pacific is equally a threat to the others." [2]

United Kingdom commitments to Australia assume flexible forms of understandings within the established traditions of the Commonwealth; nevertheless, an agreement
to maintain Australian forces in Malaya as part of a Commonwealth reserve binds Britain to the active defense of
Australian interests in New Guinea in return for the support of Malaysia against Indonesia. Behind a haze of implied commitments and loosely phrased treaty agreements,
there emerges a blunt promise by the United States and
Britain to employ their paramount force in the Pacific to
safeguard the colonial possessions as well as the mainland
of the Commonwealth of Australia. Though this may now
be accounted an accepted Western interest in the eyes of
the wielders of effective power in the region, the conditions and consequences of its implication lack public
definition. Should Australian policy toward the trust territory of New Guinea clash with majority views in the
United Nations—a by-no-means improbable contingency—
would the United States and Britain consider themselves
duty bound to support Australia even at the cost of revers-
ing the long-standing conciliation of Asian and African
nationalism? It is obvious that guarantees accorded Australia by her protectors should be matched by rights to
participate in Australian decision making in the field of
international affairs. There is little cause to question, from
a previous record of pragmatic cooperation, the willingness
of Australian statesmen to recognize obligations of partnership, even when they approach the borderline of national
sovereignty. Any claim, however, on the part of the United

States or Britain to influence Australia in her role as the largest colonial power in the area presents Australia with an equally valid right to partake in the territorial policies of her mentors. This is by no means a theoretical proposition in the light of the urgent need to bring South Seas peoples, particularly Melanesians, into forms of regional association that will make practicable their independent development. At issue lies the question of how this may be initiated while divisions are perpetuated by national colonialism—the British in the Solomons, the Australians in New Guinea and Papua, the French in New Caledonia, and the Americans in Micronesia. Australia has the clearest geographic interest and probably more experience along trade and cultural lines in dealing with the peoples of these outlying areas; if a common policy is needed for the advancement of Western interests in the region as a whole, Australian claims to act as agent for the implementation of such a policy may prove difficult to refute.

Race consciousness expressed through color prejudice is a serious handicap to recognition of Australia as an exemplar of Western interests in the Pacific realm; neither France nor the Netherlands is likely to approve doctrines of white exclusiveness. Even the United States and the United Kingdom, despite their equivocal domestic records, suffer embarrassment when the Anglo-Saxon attitude is presented as that of a racial club. The Australian position, however, bears only a surface resemblance to that of South Africa; internal minorities are not oppressed on racial grounds—the treatment of aborigines is now generally defensible and limitations on immigration are based on legitimate economic considerations as well as cultural prejudices. Originally, the Immigration Restriction Act reflected mass antagonism against non-Anglo-Saxon stock; though they were mainly directed against Chinese coolie and indentured Kanaka labor, prejudices at the time also extended to many other kinds of non-English immigrants. Thus, in the early days of the Commonwealth, a serious proposal was made to exclude Italians, with one member of the Australian Parliament pontificating that "the Italian is not civilised in the ordinary Australian sense." [3] Of course, this extreme cultural myopia has been overcome, and the whole question of color and ethnic relationship is being reexamined along rational lines. Fortunately, the initial framing of a policy of nonwhite exclusion was not enunciated in terms of racial principles. In deference to India and other members of the British Commonwealth and Empire, the first Commonwealth Parliament framed an Immigration Restriction Act based on educational qualifications rather than ethnic origins—these qualifications, one of which required proficiency in any language of the examiner's selection, were intended, and have been so used, to exclude at will all peoples of Asian origin, including Westernized Japanese. Without breaching historic safeguards, the way lies clear for public opinion to permit the entry of students, technicians, and business and cultural representatives from all parts of the world without invidious distinctions. Furthermore, the control of quantitative immigration from Asian lands for economic reasons should evoke slight challenge from newly sovereign states who have not hesitated to practice parallel restrictions in respect to their own lands.

Though New Zealand also has a highly restrictive policy on the immigration of non-Caucasians, it has been better adapted to meet obligations of the existing world situation. The acceptance of Polynesian lands as New Zealand territory—Western Samoa, the Cook, Niue, and Tokelau islands—opened the door to Polynesian immigration to the New Zealand mainland. Approximately 12,000 Polynesians settled in New Zealand between 1945 and 1962, and the movement continues at an annual rate of around 1,000. This provides a testing ground to evaluate the readiness of South Sea island inhabitants to integrate into a full-scale technological culture in accordance with Western standards. They appear to have adapted with remarkable smoothness; there have been few social conflicts, apart from some lack of the inherited Caucasian capacity to handle strong drink. An Auckland dispatch provides a concrete account of the process in an interview with Lelaulu Nonu Tuisamoa, former high chief of the Penauli district of Western Samoa.[4] Though manual labor is not in the tradition of high chiefs, Lelaulu worked as a longshoreman over a ten-year period so that he could send his sons through high school and college. His reasons for his changed way of life possess universal validity: "I came here so my children could get a good education. I want them to be something."

Accepting the social responsibility of furthering the human dignity of neighboring peoples from less-developed lands should serve to establish bonds between Anglo-Saxon and indigenous cultures that will convert geographical propinquity into an enduring union of interests. This objective may be considered the principal future contribution of the antipodean countries to a Western partnership; their strategic roles in either military or economic conflicts must necessarily be limited by their comparatively miniscule populations, which are committed to the defense of disproportionately large territories. Australian, and to a lesser degree New Zealand, policies toward peoples of neighboring, underdeveloped lands are, accordingly, of major concern to all Western powers involved in Pacific and Far Eastern affairs. Evolving methods of guiding the inhabitants of New Guinea and Papua toward a goal of political independence occupy the forefront of interest because of their scope and immediacy as a problem subject to United Nations action. Australian colonialism is conditioned, however, by the attitudes of its Western associates, Britain, France, and the United States, toward their own bordering territorial possessions. The reality of political independence for any Melanesian community, for example, largely depends upon the feasibility of a Melanesian federation or confederation embracing lands under British and French control; to a lesser degree, this is becoming equally true for Polynesian and Micronesian peoples who are at present divided by the rule of Western suzerains.

There are, therefore, two questions of paramount interest to the future of Western influence in the Pacific realm —first, the willingness of European and North American associates to recognize Australian geographic and administrative responsibilities for the development of scattered South Seas peoples and, second, the competence of the Australian state to undertake this assignment in the name of Western civilization. We can deal with the second point on a pragmatic basis by examining the previous and present administration of the most extensive colonial territory in the Pacific—Australian New Guinea and Papua. If its governmental standards and future plans for the development and support of the emerging peoples are comparable, on a lesser scale, to those undertaken by Britain, the United States, and France, Australia's geographic location as a "resident" nation could qualify it for leadership of neigh-boring communities.

When, in 1883, the then colony of Queensland annexed portions of the eastern mainland of New Guinea, the rea-sons advanced were acceptable to the nineteenth century —the need to forestall rivals on a potential military frontier. Opinion had not altered substantially by 1920 when the commonwealth was rewarded for its participation in World War I with a "C" Class League of Nations mandate over German possessions in New Guinea; until it entered the Japanese war in 1942, the Australian electorate viewed its responsibilities for the cultural and economic advancement of its Melanesian wards with considerable indifference. In this, they may be accounted no better or worse than their European exemplars in a period marked by a complacent belief in the inevitable subordination of nontechnical cul-tures. But with the transfer of the New Guinea mandate into a United Nations trusteeship and the rapid decoloni-zation of the insular and peninsular countries bordering Asia, the pendulum of governmental and public opinion swung in favor of ambitious projects for the welfare of the indigenous peoples. It is on the sincerity and success of its postwar policies that Australia should be judged as a po-tential guardian of the interests of the island peoples.

Though the distinction between the trust territory of New Guinea and the Australian territory of Papua pos-sesses international significance, they are administered as one region through the grace of a provision included in the trusteeship agreement. The New Guinea trust territory, which lies north of Papua, covers some 93,000 square miles in which nature has created formidable barriers to access and easy communication; swampy coastlands lead up through ravines and cliffs to an area of rain forests that guard one of the greatest mountain ranges in the world. Of the population of approximately 1,500,000 indigenous inhabitants and 16,000 Australians and Chinese, 50 percent dwell in the three coastal zones and 44 percent in the highlands; the remaining 6 percent are dispersed in adjoining islands. By no stretch of the imagination may the indigenous inhabitants be regarded as a united nation; the physical separation is matched by a disparity of language, estimated at around 700 different tongues. An agricultural economy, based on local needs, produces cash crops for export largely around centers of population and through the efforts of nonindigenous residents. Alienation of the land, however, has never been extensive and has now virtually ceased. In the late 1920's, gold was discovered there, and equipment had to be transported by air and required a substantial capital investment. Recently, mining by the indigenous people has increased; they now contribute 12 percent of total gold production. From both an economic and a cultural point of view, the territory is clearly dependent on external organization, and its social problems can be solved only through administrative and political means.

The trust territory of New Guinea and the contiguous Australian territory of Papua share a joint administrative system. Executive, and to some extent legislative, authority resides in an Administrator, appointed by and responsible to the Minister of State for Territories of the Commonwealth of Australia. The central administrative structure has seventeen departments; they deal with such matters as public health, agriculture, forestry, lands, education, native affairs, and law. Administration in the field is carried out through districts, nine in New Guinea and fifteen in Papua. These districts are staffed by the Territory Public Service, which is recruited from British subjects and Australian "protected persons"—a classification that opens the ranks to qualified Melanesians and Papuans. Major questions affecting the governmental structure are the degree of representation to be granted the indigenous majority; the relationship between central and district governments, and the practicality of training indigenous personnel to replace the Australian administrative staff. These issues are obviously interlocked, and they must be solved simultaneously if social chaos is to be avoided. Fortunately, the Australian government has been stimulated by the reports of a series of United Nations visiting missions to make constitutional and political advances; recommendations by the 1962 visiting mission for the creation of a truly representative legislature were almost immediately accepted by the government at Canberra.

Participation in their own government through representative institutions involves the indigenous peoples in problems of national identity as well as in technical questions relating to the conduct of elections. Tribal groups speaking some 700 different tongues and only recently in effective contact with one another have to appraise the degree and nature of social union desired. An interview between John Guise, a native New Guinean who is leader of the elected members of the House of Assembly, and Gerald Lyons of the Australian Broadcasting Commission throws light on how this issue is being faced:

> LYONS: They are the people you represent. Now what do these people want? What about the people

who are not highly developed or are still in the tribal state and live simple and almost primitive lives? These people are almost inarticulate, aren't they, in their wants? . . . What do you feel you have in common with these people—the under-developed people you represent—what do you feel you have in common?

GUISE: The thing that we have in common is that we are the people of the country.

LYONS: This is a racial thing? Or a national feeling?

GUISE: It is, I think, a national feeling.

LYONS: Not a racial feeling?

GUISE: No. . . . I look upon my duty in Papua–New Guinea as one playing his small part toward the over-all development of Papua–New Guinea. And I look upon it as solemn duty. . . . I have been elected by my people, it is my duty to help as much as possible—and be loyal to my mother country.[5]

In response to the conclusion of the 1962 United Nations visiting mission "that the whole Territory must be drawn together and given the means for free political expression by the creation of a representative parliament," the Australian government scheduled a general election based on a common roll and single-member constituencies for April, 1964. Intensive educational work on the district level ensured, to a considerable measure, that the issues involved and the electoral process in general were understood. Results were highly satisfactory, with an estimated 68.9 percent of the qualified electorate going to the polls. A surprising development was the number of Europeans elected from overwhelmingly indigenous constituencies; to provide a backbone of experience, provision had been made for the inclusion of twenty Europeans in a legislature of sixty-four members. Ten European civil servants were to be nominated and ten Europeans elected from specially-drawn European constituencies. In the forty-four constituencies with indigenous majorities, however, six European candidates topped the polls, a heartening tribute to the friendly relations existing in the coffee-growing regions of the highlands. The executive power in the territory still resides in the Administration. An Administrator's Council has been constituted with a nonofficial majority appointed from, but not elected by, the House of Assembly. Though the functions of this council are advisory, the Administrator is bound to explain his reasons to the House of Assembly should he disregard their advice.

The new constitution is a prelude to, rather than an assertion of, self-government, for a reserved power to veto legislation is retained by the government at Canberra. Nevertheless, an almost irreversible political momentum toward eventual independence has been put in motion. The government of Australia has declared that independence is its objective despite the risk that Papua–New Guinea nationhood may embrace the whole island area, and bring Australia into direct competition with Indonesia in West Irian for the future guidance of the region. Credit must be accorded the government and people of Australia for an imaginative advance toward the development of Melanesian nationalism, even though they may have been spurred in part by the fear of being forestalled by Indonesia. Australia's achievement will depend, however, upon her willingness and capacity to fulfill the aroused expectations of the indigenous peoples for the material progress and educational training needed to unite these underdeveloped communities into a truly self-governing nation. Future promises for the establishment of a University College in New Guinea and for intensified economic development may be set against a doubtful record of parsimonious neglect over past decades.[6]

Criticism of Australian administration in United Nations Trusteeship Council debates in 1962 centered around a lack of educational facilities and a suspicion of exploitation by Australian corporate interests. The Soviet delegate pointed out that only .01 percent of New Guinean youths were receiving secondary education at that time, and the delegate from Liberia noted the failure of the Australian administration to prepare any substantial number of New Guineans for university education in order to qualify them for senior posts in the administration of their own country. In respect to economic discrimination, wage scales paying New Guinean labor less than one-seventh of the wages paid corresponding Australian workers elicited condemnation. Essentially, criticism was directed at previous failures of the colonial administration to stimulate social progress; but a lack of evidence of substantial discontent among the indigenous peoples or of any desire to withdraw from Australian tutelage blunted the rhetoric of anticolonial nations.

The posture of Australia in Papua–New Guinea may now be considered to satisfy enlightened Western standards of the proper relationship between technologically developed and underdeveloped peoples. Doubt remains, however, as to whether the limited economic and technical resources of Australia will be enough to fulfill, within a safe margin of time, the obligations undertaken. Capital, in terms of skills and educational facilities as well as money, will be required in hitherto unprecedented quantities to guide Papua–New Guinea into the standards of a Western-oriented, independent state. The limited population of Australia has difficulty enough in developing its vast mainland territories with surpluses from its free enterprise system; raising the standard of living in Papua–New Guinea to a level where Western-style democracy would become practicable is clearly not a profitable enterprise for the Australian economy. There are, of course, other considerations that might weigh with the Australian people when they contemplate this task—factors relating to Australia's ultimate place in the Pacific realm and the degree of support she may receive from North American and European nations. If Australia is to be the standard-bearer of a Western system among the island peoples of the Pacific, entrusted with the major economic and political direction of their development, she must be assured of lasting and effective cooperation from her Western associates. Not only will petty claims to national sovereignty over Pacific possessions have to be resolved in her favor, or dissolved through some international protectorate, but she must be given substantial control over the planning of Western developmental contributions for the advancement of Pacific peoples. The reluctance of European and North American nations to pool territorial and other interests in the Pacific realm and place them under the supervision of the antipodean countries may be offset by the lack of alternatives open to directionless and squabbling Westerners in the face of emergent Pacific nationalism, which is being exploited by Communist China and expansionist Indonesia. Though sweeping gestures toward Australian hegemony over Pacific possessions are outside practical politics, immediate policies can be framed to assure the Australian nation that sacrifices to maintain a Western "presence" in Papua–New Guinea will be viewed as a cooperative enterprise by, at least, her British and American allies.

Among the most inviting of such potential policies is a joint effort to further development of a United States of Melanesia, encompassing Papua–New Guinea, the British Solomons, the New Hebrides, and, at a later stage, Indonesian West Irian and France's New Caledonia. This gathering together of peoples of Melanesian origin would provide a more stable base for political independence and at the same time enlarge frontiers of association with more advanced Pacific communities such as Fiji. As a Melanesian federation would require initially joint sponsorship by the Anglo-Saxon powers, responsibility for its economic and social development could be shared in a manner that would render the burden practicable for all concerned. Through mutual concessions in regard to technical sovereignty, Australia and Britain could inaugurate a United States of Melanesia—as has been advocated by responsible Australian scholars[7]—at any time. In practice, however, substantial support from the United States would be required to disencumber the respective governments from their traditional colonial attitudes. Although the United States may be reluctant to engage itself in the future of these faraway peoples, a Western failure to grasp the initiative would provide Indonesia with the opportunity to infiltrate all Pacific island possessions of the West. A Melanesian federation would be a training ground for future federal organization of the main groups among the Pacific peoples. Modern communications and technology render evolution of wider political forms almost inevitable;

the only question is who will preside over the birth of these new nation groups in the most sensitive area of Western influence in the Pacific.

New Zealand's position in Pacific affairs has received insufficient recognition from Western associates who are dazzled by the grand strategies of power politics. Neither fleets nor nuclear missiles are capable of organizing the peoples dwelling in the Pacific islands into modern communities. Lacking such organization, the vast area of the Pacific Ocean is doomed to remain "occupied territory," garrisoned by Western nations to protect their lines of communication now that half the world has fallen into hostile hands. Partnership in progress as well as security remains in the rhetorical stage, with the major metropolitan powers of the West relegating the housekeeping task of "administering the natives" to dedicated, but lower, echelons of their civil services.

New Zealand's assimilation of the strongest and most cohesive element of Polynesian culture, the Maori people, its administration of Western Samoa, the Cook and Tokelau islands, and Niue makes it responsible for the destiny of nearly half the peoples of Polynesian origin. This has been glossed over as a factor in the maintenance of Western influence throughout the Pacific realm. As administering authority, New Zealand granted independence to the 100,000 Polynesians of Western Samoa in 1962. This marked the first milestone on the road to political sovereignty for Pacific island peoples. To some extent, this leap forward embarrasses other Western colonial powers in the region—the United States, Britain, and France—by demonstrating the capacity of a small island population to control its own affairs in the dignity of independence. Though in the first half of the twentieth century New Zealand rule encountered a stormy passage, the resolute resistance of the indigenous Mau movement served to create an atmosphere of mutual respect that led to political severance in terms of national consciousness. Of course, Western Samoans are still a dependent people insofar as their defense remains a New Zealand responsibility and their economic viability is linked to the generosity of that state. Nevertheless, this condition is viewed on both sides as a temporary expedient occasioned by the failure of the Western powers to organize regional groups of Pacific peoples that would permit them to project their cultural heritage into the world of present-day technology. The efforts of the New Zealand government to further Pacific regionalism, since its initiation along with Australia of the South Pacific Commission, have made slight impression on the strategy-dominated preoccupations of their Western associates. The creation of a self-governing Pacific island state, however minute, demonstrates that such political cells can exist as building blocks for larger bodies. The continuance of direct colonial rule over similar possessions may henceforth be justified by Western nations only on the grounds that confederation plans are politically, economically, and technically impracticable in the region.

In the light of its successful partnership with Samoa, New Zealand's policies in the Cook and Tokelau islands and in Niue deserve consideration. Lying 1,800 miles northeast of New Zealand, the Cook group of fifteen islands provides a living space of 93 square miles for approximately 18,400 Polynesians, who are closely related to the Maoris. An economy based on tropical fruits and copra does not suffice to support progressive social needs; more than half the public revenue is contributed by New Zealand. Economic dependency notwithstanding, self-government through a popularly elected Legislative Assembly has operated since 1958. Government service is staffed in a ratio of more than 8 to 1 in favor of local residents over New Zealand personnel. Primary education is compulsory, and there is a college-level institution, principally for teacher education, at Ratonga, the capital. Cooperative societies have been fostered to the point where their membership comprises 3,000 out of a total of less than 5,000 working adult males. Small industrial plants, of which the most important is a processing plant for fruit juice, have been established on the basis of a New Zealand market for their products. Among the more enlightened policies of New Zealand has been the provision of scholarships to Western Samoa and to New Zealand itself; moreover, the nation's hospitable attitude toward mainland migration has permitted a measure of relief from population pressure. There can be little question that association with New Zealand has opened the door to social progress on Western terms without inflicting penalties on the cultural dignity of the inhabitants or denying them substantial control over their own affairs.

In October, 1964, the government of New Zealand proposed a further step toward full internal self-government for the Cook islanders, which became operative in 1965.[8] All governmental matters, except those relating to defense and external affairs, became the exclusive province of the indigenous legislature and administration. However, New Zealand's Minister of Island Territories remains as adviser, though relinquishing claims to legal control. Cook islanders resident in New Zealand—numbering between one-quarter and one-third of the island's people—have been given a form of dual citizenship that permits them to participate in the public affairs of whichever country they reside in for more than one year. This sensible arrangement satisfies the spirit of the 1960 United Nations resolution calling for the immediate independence of all non-self-governing territories without ignoring the Cook islanders' continuing need for military protection and economic support.

A general election held in April, 1965, with a United Nations team acting as observers, resulted in the Cook Islands party winning fourteen of the twenty-two Assembly seats. In general, this party favors acceptance of the proposed constitution with minor amendments.

Niue, an isolated island lying between Tonga and the Cook Islands, supports less than 5,000 inhabitants on meager agricultural resources. Population pressure has been alleviated to some extent, however, by migration of over 1,000 Niueans to New Zealand during the past decade. Despite a New Zealand subsidy that outweighs local revenue, the Niue Island Assembly has, since 1961, possessed control over all expenditures, except those set aside for economic development by the New Zealand donor. Scholarships to New Zealand, Western Samoa, and Fiji maintain an educational link with the rest of the region.

The Tokelau Islands, with a population of under 2,000, are a group of atolls some 300 miles north of Western Samoa. The islands were formerly administered from Samoa, and the close connection has been maintained after Western Samoan independence, with the New Zealand administrator continuing to reside in Apia, and members of the Samoan government paying frequent visits to the outlying group. Political federation with Samoa awaits only a realistic solution of the question as to who is in a position to bear the costs.

New Zealand's posture toward Pacific island peoples is in many ways the most enlightened of all Westernized nations. Her government and people have recognized that the capacity of small island communities to manage their own political affairs indicates that a regional organization for all South Seas peoples would be practicable. But New Zealand is incapable of achieving this from her own resources. Consequently, she is compelled to bear the economic and administrative burden of the arrested development of peoples entrusted to her care. Nevertheless, she has made a significant contribution to Western influence in the Pacific realm by demonstrating the practicality of generous and far-seeing policies that are at present blocked elsewhere mainly through the faltering indecision of her more powerful European and North American associates.

8 • THE TERRITORIAL
STAKE OF
THE UNITED STATES

The right of the United States to participate in Far Eastern affairs rests on the reality of its presence as a Pacific power. (See map, pp. 4–5.) A western seaboard, whose defense requires that the North Pacific be controlled as a virtual American lake, provides one basis for United States intervention in power struggles throughout the region. Military necessity, however, is a negative aspect of American involvement, which should be more properly centered on social and economic developments pioneered by its own citizens. It is neither the western littoral nor Alaska that qualifies the United States as a leader among Pacific peoples but rather Hawaii, whose entry into the Union in the full dignity of statehood reduced barriers of cultural and ethnic origin that separated inhabitants of the continental United States from the polyglot people of

Asia and the Pacific. This should be accounted more than a sentimental gesture, because the record of Hawaii presents solid evidence that individuals of differing cultural origins can be compatible when they are given access to a common technological and political environment. American nationalism as a culture symbol has proved itself capable of expanding among mixed ethnic groups if conditions are favorable to the cultivation of skills and advanced technology. Guam repeats the Hawaiian experience in miniature, and the likelihood that this experience will expand throughout the Pacific island chains is limited more by the practicability of technological advances than by cultural barriers.

Despite ethnic prejudice, deep-rooted within aging and presumably passing power circles in the continental United States, Americans have already taken steps in the direction of becoming a Pacific as well as an Atlantic people. Because Communist China is promoting an ideological "Chinese wall" between Caucasian and non-Caucasian races—yellow, brown, and black—Western strategy should devise a counterbid for human solidarity within an advancing world culture of technology.

The strategic concerns of the United States suffer from their dual nature, which has not been sufficiently clarified. The traditional defense of the continental western coast extending as far as Hawaii predates the Japanese war and is based on concepts of exclusive control of areas of the Pacific Ocean, concepts that are still valid despite developments in missile warfare. On the other hand, the victory over Japan left a power vacuum in Southeast Asia and the Far East that was tempting to communist aggression; therefore, we had to step in and use our military power. In this respect, the United States has acted as a champion of world, or more accurately Western, order with its own needs of continental defense in a secondary role. Policies, both military and political, had to be devised on a pragmatic basis in the face of unpredictable events and the lack of any generally accepted design for a future world order. It is in this area that United States strategic interests must be constantly revised until some lasting establishment of social purpose as an end common to all. In the words of a British Air marshal, commenting on the effectiveness of the SEATO treaty, "if prosperity and stability are the real interests of the Western Powers in this area, then the Treaty's military provisions should be paralleled by massive and effective support for economic development through channels acceptable to the countries whom it has sought to assist." [1] Prior to the Vietnam involvement the United States had contributed $5 billion, heavily weighted toward military assistance.

Strategic regionalism may serve as a summarization of shifting American policies. Empires, whether relics of European dominion, Japanese ambition, or communist aggression were to be replaced by associations of free peoples organized as independent nations. Though transition has proved neither easy nor wholly successful, no alternative objective appears compatible with the long-run security of the American people themselves. Progressively, a Western commitment has been made to at least defend the freedom of the small countries of peninsular and insular Asia from external aggression. To withdraw now would ensure the extension of communist influence and control over most of the Far East and a substantial part of the Pacific basin. It would be inadequate compensation should the communist giants of China and Soviet Russia fight over the ensuing spoils. Prognostications from a bookish study concerning the future shape of specific United States policies are of scant value. What is under consideration in this writing is the base that underpins and must inevitably limit American operations of any character in this region. Three aspects may be attributed to any operational base for United States Far Eastern and Pacific policy; in the first place, there is an occupational aspect in terms of the area, whether land or sea, fully under control for purposes of military deployment and supply. Second, a diplomatic-military base has developed from alliances and agreements involving military assistance or the use of other nations' military installations. Finally, policy must rest on political and social objectives that are acceptable to, or capable of being imposed upon, all participating elements.

With regard to the occupational feature, United States government agencies, from Congress and the President downward, have lacked candor with their own people and the outside world. Island possessions, such as Guam, those of the strategic trust territories, and probably Okinawa, remain indispensable, if not to the narrow defense of our shores, certainly to the military posture essential to our total security and world aims. To equivocate concerning the nature of our occupation of these areas, maintaining that the connection is that of transient guardianship until the inhabitants are advanced enough to choose their own future, appears a profitless deception. It would be more honorable, and probably more rewarding, to admit our needs and accord the peoples concerned the dignity of full and equal association in return for the military use of their lands. In this respect, a lesson may be learned from the comparative results of the treatment meted out to Puerto Rico and Cuba during the first decades of the twentieth century.

The reality of American Guam serves as a focus for United States intentions of extending its national territory into the Far Pacific. There are three conceivable futures open for Guam: independence with a consequent renunciation of United States citizenship by the Guamanians; indefinite existence as a garrison outpost wholly dependent on the continental mainland for its economic, political, and social development; and, finally, the transformation of Guam into a commonwealth of Pacific islands through the voluntary adhesion of Micronesian components at present under strategic trust and perhaps future association of such groups as the Gilbert and Ellice chain. Independence, potentially catastrophic to the island's economy, would amount to a flagrant betrayal of American citizens who are entitled to the preservation of acquired American standards and the protection of their government. Besides, the separation of Guam from the United States would reduce our commitment in the Pacific to that of a distant military striking force. The present compromise of a garrison community, however, is politically and socially unstable, for it restricts Guamanian prospects for development and invites justified criticism from powerful neighbors such as Indonesia and the Philippine Republic. For the most part, it is a consequence of Congressional inertia, abetted by military fears of alterations in the political status quo that might make the use of Guamanian territory and manpower inconvenient.

The island of Guam, 6,000 miles southwest of San Francisco and 1,500 miles southeast of Manila, covers an area of 209 square miles and supports a total population of over 66,000. More than one-third of the residents are continental Americans, principally military personnel and their dependents. The indigenous Guamanians parallel Hawaiians in their admixture of Chamorro, Spanish, Filipino, Okinawan, Japanese, and American strains. One-third of the island's land is reserved for the operation of one of the most important military bases of the United States in the Pacific. Guamanian livelihood is tied to a wage economy that is based, in general, on the requirements of the military —in recent years, barely 4 percent of the labor force has been engaged in commercial agriculture.

In constitutional terms, Guam is an unincorporated territory of the United States, governed by the Organic Act of 1950, which provides a measure of local legislative autonomy and grants United States citizenship to Guamanians. The shadow of the Northwest Ordinance of 1787, which established the pattern of territorial government on the bases of a separation of powers and a system of checks and balances, obfuscates the present political structure of Guam. An unimaginative application of traditional mainland devices to the rule of a Pacific outpost has needlessly complicated the current political scene. The separation of executive and legislative functions operates satisfactorily enough when both organs of government are subject to the same master—a sovereign electorate. Under dependency conditions, however, though the legislative body may be locally elected and controlled, the executive is appointed by the metropolitan government to act as their agent in reconciling the policies of the national government with the opinions of the local population. This arrangement either denigrates local self-government or deprives the central government of residual control according to the tempera-ment of the governor or the passion of the legislature. In any case, a lack of responsibility to a single political master prevents the mutual interchange essential to proper func-tioning of the operational aspects of government. Guam is confined in a political web with an appointed Governor serving as executive for the elected Legislature. A recent concession toward greater island autonomy has been the appointment by Washington of a Guamanian, Manuel S. L. Guerrero, to the office of Governor—a precedent that may foreshadow the choice of a Governor through popular election.

Local government operates through a more closely in-tegrated system. Nineteen administrative districts are each headed by an elected Commissioner or Mayor, with a Chief Commissioner, appointed for a four-year term by the Governor on the advice of the Legislature, who coordi-nates relations between the local governments and the central administration. At this level, local self-government functions smoothly in accordance with the joint will of the local and all island electorates.

Political government in Guam would be enhanced in ac-cordance with mainland standards if federal suzerainty were represented through a High Commissioner, on the British model, who would remain responsible for the supervision of strictly federal expenditures and the maintenance of na-tional prerogatives, including a veto power over laws passed by the Guamanian legislature. For the direction of intraisland affairs, an executive directly responsible to the legislature and electorate on a parliamentary basis would restore substantial control over their own concerns to the people of the island. As Guamanians lack direct representation in Congress, the government of the United States, for all its goodwill and generosity, remains an alien power. This needless and frustrating complication of the government structure in Guam stems from the preservation of jealously guarded anachronisms within the national government itself. The Department of the Interior, entombing the Office of Territories, has the competence of a narrow-minded hen entrusted with the rearing of adventurous ducklings. In terms of its bureaucratic pattern, Interior is parochial, acutely responsive to pressures of mainland interest groups, and indifferent to matters touching on the United States external position in the world. This policy vacuum is compounded by the powerful congressional committees that serve as watch dogs over the department's affairs. The House of Representatives Committee for Interior Affairs permits its Insular Affairs Subcommittee a certain degree of freedom in drafting legislation and proposing expenditures. Despite a gallant struggle over the last decade by the subcommittee's Democratic chairman, Representative Leo W. O'Brien of New York, every concession has to be wrung out of the massive indifference of the main body, reflecting it must be said in all fairness an even greater lack of interest on the part of the majority of the members of the House.

Policy making for the Pacific lands occupied by the United States will remain crippled until a greater degree of elementary administrative coordination is achieved. In the first place, the status of the Office of Territories should be changed so that, wherever it is placed in the administrative design, it would be in a position to coordinate the policies of the State Department, Defense, and other bureaucratic monoliths insofar as they touch on territorial affairs, particularly in regard to the flow of technical and financial assistance from all the varied sources of the federal apparatus. Guam, for example, is a member of the international South Pacific Commission, a body possessing the potential to plan, integrate, and supply assistance for research and technical purposes to the peoples of the Pacific island chains. Yet representation of the United States on this vital economic commission is channeled through the Pacific desk of the State Department with only informal contact with the Office of Territories. Likewise, educational and training facilities with which the United States might make a serious bid to attract the loyalties of emerging Pacific peoples are under the aegis of the State Department—not Territories—in the Center for Cultural and Technical Interchange between East and West (the East-West Center) attached to the University of Hawaii. It may be expected that findings of the study of commonwealth status inaugurated for Puerto Rico will eventually affect the archaic organization for the administration of territories. The waiting period, however, may prove costly to United States prestige both in the eyes of her own dependent peoples and in the opinion of the emerging nations of Asia and Africa.

The economy of Guam represents a triumph of recovery from man-made and natural catastrophes. During the Japanese war, Agana, the capital, and many of the northern coastal villages were destroyed along with coconut plantations and village holdings, thus forcing a dispersal of the population. As restitution was a clear responsibility of the mainland government, a planning commission was established to implement both the rebuilding of Agana and a relocation program. In the field of economic development, the Guam Finance and Development Agency, constituted in 1951, became responsible for credit facilities and research activities to assist agriculture, industry, construction, commerce, and housing. A Guam Farm Finance Corporation utilizes a revolving fund of $300,000 to encourage the revival of agriculture. A civilian payroll of the United States Navy in the neighborhood of $12 million, of which around $4 million represents direct pay checks to Guamanians, underpins the wage economy. The net result is a relatively high standard of living for the region; as of 1957, a family of five had an average income of almost $3,000. Public finance since the Organic Act of 1950 has been based on such sources as federal income taxes and customs duties, which are paid directly into the treasury of the territory. The income tax, derived substantially from the comparatively well-paid third of the residents in the armed services of the United States, represents the principal source of revenue. Under these conditions, government revenue normally suffices to meet the administrative costs of the island communities. When natural disasters occur, such as the typhoon of 1963, Guam receives direct assistance from the national government.

Education, after a slow start during the prewar period of Navy administration, is still handicapped by a shortage of skilled teachers. Vocational and higher education, barely sufficing to meet the growing needs of the local inhabitants, is inadequate to face the challenge of a center for American influence among Pacific island peoples. Though a four-year college has now replaced a former two-year establishment, it would appear wholly unrealistic to expect Guam to use its own educational skills and financial resources to establish American supremacy in training Pacific peoples for modern conditions of life. A center for Pacific island peoples adequate to supply the educational skills needed to transform the area into a technological environment would be only a minor burden for the United States, at least in comparison with the costly supervision of unending counterinsurgency struggles absorbing men and money in peninsular Asia. In light of the harsh necessity of preserving a stable social base among the Pacific islands if we are to maintain meaningful military strength, preventive action to forestall antagonistic influences appears to be elementary strategy. In the meantime, Guam, which should be the exemplar of what the technological culture of North America has to offer, has been sending students to the attenuated medical school at Suva, in British Fiji, to meet its own requirements for medical skills.

Guamanian politics appear to have attained a dead center of comparative calm with little of the social tensions bedeviling other garrison areas such as the Canal Zone of Panama. The loyalty of the Guamanians as participating citizens is an undervalued asset of our nation in the Far Pacific. Their adaptability to, and acceptance of, American standards proves more effectively than ideological arguments the suitability of Western mores to the task of easing the transition of island communities into a technological environment. Expansion of Western-oriented societies has become practical through the power of attraction: the magnets of education, skills, and patterns of trade are replacing political dominance. The initiative, however, rests with the United States; neither the islanders themselves nor the exhausted colonialism of Europe possesses the physical means to control transition. It is regrettable that the strategic value of North American cultural influence remains obscured by the fascination of military interventions and the hidden remnants of race prejudice.

Guam and the adjacent Saipan provide a naval and air base for the United States that is essential to securing the lines of communication to Australia and New Zealand. The military worth of other islands in the Caroline strategic trust area probably varies with changing concepts in the Pentagon and is not open to public debate. The missile base at Kwajalein in the Marshall Islands is maintained as a tightly guarded security preserve. Indigenous employees are not permitted to reside on the island, which has been sumptuously outfitted to accommodate United States personnel and their dependents. The neighboring island of Ebeye has been transformed into a dormitory for commuting workers. A population increase on the island from 300 to 3,400 since 1946 occasioned squalid and unsanitary living conditions, which were tardily and inadequately rectified.

United States acceptance of a strategic trust obligates its government in the eyes of the rest of the world to treat the inhabitants of this region as if they were making a substantial contribution to the defense of the metropolitan country. A strategic trust is based on the assumption of the overriding importance of national defense and the preservation of world order as against the cultural and political freedom of the indigenous inhabitants. Fortification of the area, with the consequent perils and restrictions imposed on the localities, represents the degree to which indigenous interests are subordinated to metropolitan necessities. The responsibility for seeing that the American advantages are balanced with a concern for the future of the Micronesian and Polynesian peoples involved has been disregarded by the Congress of the United States. As a natural enough re-action against the cost in United States blood and treasure expended in the capture of these lands from the Japanese, Congress has, by and large, rested American claims on the fact of conquest. An ignoble parsimony, based on indifference to planning for the integration of its wards in some form of Pacific development, has crippled the conscience of the holders of the public purse. The Kennedy Administration, stung by outspoken criticism in the United Nations, increased the miserly $7 million annual budget for civil administration to $17.5 million. Further, a presidential commission, headed by Arthur M. Solomon, later Assistant Secretary of State for Economic Affairs, made an intensive survey of the territory in 1963. The report of the Solomon committee is presumed to have contained suggestions such as the employment of Peace Corps volunteers in Micronesia that are now being implemented. For security reasons, perhaps relating to the good name of the United States in the United Nations and inconvenient domestic criticism, the whole of the Solomon report has been declared confidential.

Under the Johnson Administration, further steps have been taken to fulfill minimum obligations to the Micronesian islanders. In May, 1966, Congress was asked to raise the annual budget for civilian administration to $22 million for 1967, with a progressive increase to $38 million by 1971. In addition, a capital investment budget of $172 million for health, education, transportation, water, sewage disposal, and other services was requested. The previous attitude of the House Appropriations Committee, under the chairmanship of Wayne N. Aspinall, Democrat of Colorado, was consistently hostile to increased spending in

Micronesia. As of February, 1967, Congress had not yet approved the increased appropriations requested by the President.

The report of the United Nations Visiting Mission to the Trust Territory of the Pacific Islands in 1964 evaluates the achievements of United States administration in the following terms:

> Perhaps because the money is not available the Administration has so far had to devise piecemeal programs in the economic field and has not engaged in over-all economic planning or a co-ordinated campaign to stimulate the entire Micronesian economy. This may be one reason why only piecemeal progress has been made in mobilizing the ideas and energies of the people of Micronesia in the considerable task of helping them to stand on their own economic feet.[2]

Of course, natural obstacles in the way of the social and economic advancement of these scattered peoples are numerous and may not be removed in any manner likely to prove profitable to the United States economy. Dependency, both economic and cultural, is an unavoidable consequence of American occupation. It is regrettable that so inadequate an advertisement of American reciprocity toward peoples conscripted into her national defense system should be maintained in the center of the Pacific realm. Perhaps an unresolved dichotomy between needs of our military arm that have not been fully disclosed and the parochialism of an insufficiently informed Congress contributes to our loss of prestige in this instance. The executive side of the national government has proved more responsive in its selection of dedicated second-level administrators[3] and through its efforts to make sense out of a cumbersome bureaucratic machinery that should be thoroughly reorganized along budgetary and administrative lines.

The islands forming the Trust Territory are grouped into three archipelagos that are loosely grouped together as Micronesia—the Marianas, the Carolines, and the Marshalls—though the British Gilbert and Ellice group and Guam itself fall within boundaries of an ethnographic Micronesia. There are a total of 2,141 islands spread over 3 million square miles of the western Pacific Ocean; the land area of 700 square miles provides living space for about 90,000 inhabitants. For administrative purposes, the area is divided into six districts, each under a district administrator, that vary in population from 6,000 in Yap to 21,500 in Truk. The High Commissioner, under the direction of the Secretary of the Interior, vests in his person the executive and legislative authority for the Trust Territory. This classic colonial framework of government is tempered by the objectives and practices of a well-intentioned metropolis. In the words of the Department of State 1963 Annual Report on the Trust Territory of the Pacific Islands:

> It is the policy of the Administering Authority and of the Trust Territory Government to foster and promote political development toward self-government or independence. Through educational programs and technical advice every effort is made to develop understanding by the people of the features of democracy so that they can make an informed and meaningful decision as to those aspects to be made applicable in the Territory. These efforts are particularly important because of the necessity

of developing democratic structures, institutions, and procedures to enable the people to meet the challenges of the modern world. That the people of the Territory are meeting this challenge is seen by the greatly accelerated pace of movement toward self-government during the period covered in this report.[4]

District autonomy is well organized through island congresses. An account of that of Truk, the most populous of all the islands, may serve to illustrate the pattern. Since 1957, Truk has had a unicameral District Congress with representatives elected from each municipality for a three-year term. The function of this body is primarily to handle a local budget and make regulations for community programs. Municipalities, of which Truk has thirty, constitute the bulk of administrative units throughout Micronesia. Generally they are based on the boundaries of traditional chieftainships, allowing a transition from a former hereditary principle to elective leadership. Executive heads of municipalities, normally termed magistrates, are elected to office with the choice often falling on some member of a chiefly family. An ambitious move to establish a Council of Micronesia was inaugurated in 1961. This body of twelve members, two elected from each district by universal suffrage, is advisory in character. Steps to convert the council into a territorial legislature or Congress of Micronesia reached the stage of a draft Executive Order in 1964.

In the summer of 1965, a bicameral Congress of Micronesia was convened at Saipan. The House of Delegates was composed of two members from each of the six districts, and the General Assembly, totaling twenty-two members, represented the districts proportionately to population. The 1964 United Nations Visiting Mission to the Trust Territory of the Pacific Islands commented on the function of the Congress in the following terms:

> the Mission has formed the strong impression that Micronesia is now welding itself into a unified people. The conditions exist in which rapid political development becomes both possible and necessary. . . . The essence of political development is the assumption by the people of Micronesia of control over their own affairs. The means are the creation of a strong Micronesian legislature and an executive controlled, and as far as possible staffed, by Micronesians. The Mission accepts the view that progress may not be made equally rapidly on both these fronts; it believes that the legislature, through the inauguration of the Congress of Micronesia, offers the quickest way of securing an effective Micronesian participation in the process of government. If, however, the Congress of Micronesia is to be the effective voice and instrument of Micronesian wishes, it must have real powers, particularly over finance, and the organization and means to exercise those powers.[5]

Despite problems of distance, diversity, and lack of resources, the constitutional theory, respectably related to that of the American Congress established under the Articles of Confederation, appears admirable. Political machinery, however, requires the fuel of an avowed purpose held in common to permit proper operation. When Micronesians assemble together the first question confronting them—"to what political community do we belong?"—is answerable only by their political suzerain, the United States, which has clearly not reached any decision on the matter. Lacking a definite prospect of United States citizenship in some commonwealth form or, alternatively, independence or association with some outside federation or confederation, it is difficult to see how Micronesian representatives can agree to the nature or purpose of a political union. A discussion club to get acquainted and to elevate the dialogue with their metropolitan master is the most that may be reasonably expected from this infant body. It may be noted that in an attempt to obtain a "grass roots" response from the indigenous inhabitants—a plebiscite held in Saipan in 1961—out of a total of 2,847 registered voters, 2,517 voted their desire to become United States citizens, either through unification with Guam or as a separate territory, and only 27 indicated a preference for the status quo. According to the 1964 visiting mission,

> the people of the Territory have not begun to think at all widely about the range of alternatives open to them. Almost all speakers assumed that there were only two alternatives—full independence or some form of integration with the United States. Independence is taken to mean that Micronesia would have to stand entirely on its own strength and that United States aid would immediately cease. Since Micronesia is clearly not self-sufficient most concluded that the only alternative was some form of integration with the United States, either as part of Hawaii or part of the Territory of Guam.[6]

Though in 1963 the High Commissioner had at his disposal for economic and social development an appropriation 100 percent greater than in the previous year, the lag in opening up the islands to the standards of technological culture continues to react against belief in the good faith of the United States among emergent nations in Asia and Africa. During Trusteeship Council debates at the thirtieth session of the United Nations in 1963, the Soviet delegate outlined some possible lines of attack on vulnerable United States attitudes in this area. Though the United States had subscribed to the United Nations declaration on the granting of independence to colonial countries and peoples, it had declined to accede to requests of the Trusteeship Council to inform the Security Council, as supervising body of a strategic trust, of any target dates for independence. Further, the Soviet spokesman suggested that the United States was trying to make the territory inaccessible and to make the Pacific an American sea by preventing the development of friendly relations between its inhabitants and those of neighboring countries. Granted that our world adversaries will utilize the slenderest hooks on which to display distrust of American good faith, still the United States government has needlessly exposed itself to suspicion through its failure to be honest with itself and with the rest of the world on its plans for its Micronesian wards. If our military posture permits us to free these islands from occupation, definite plans for political independence should be proclaimed; if not, then honest acceptance of the inhabitants as fellow Americans in return for the risks they run on our military frontier appears the least honor requires of a powerful nation.

A clearer confession of strategic necessity may be found in the United States occupation of Okinawa in the Ryuku island chain, following upon a security treaty negotiated in conjunction with the Japanese peace treaty and revised in 1960. Though the United States recognizes Japan's "residual sovereignty" in Okinawa, and has in fact returned northern islands in the Ryuku chain to Japanese administration, our avowed intention is to remain in occupation as long as there is a threat to the free people of Asia. In stricter terms of international law, our military possession will be justified at least over the ten-year period contemplated by the revised security treaty of 1960. From a realistic viewpoint, the value of the base will depend on the capacity of the United States administration to placate the 900,000 Okinawans sufficiently to avoid widespread communist subversion or a growth of the *Hon-Do* movement aimed at a reversion to Japanese rule.

Present and future significance of this military outpost, 500 miles from the eastern Chinese coast, is well evidenced. In the early months of 1964, a military exercise airlifting 4,000 troops from Hawaii to Okinawa with a refueling stop at Guam was successfully completed.[7] Military power, however, should always take into account the inherent transitoriness of political arrangements, particularly when they affect bases with a civilian population that is not integrated with the social and political society of the armed personnel. Success in maintaining Okinawa as a military stronghold up to the present time stems from two sources —first, the dependency of Japan on American military protection and economic goodwill, and, second, on the generous administrative policies adopted during the last few years within Okinawa itself. In respect to the social pattern achieved, the income of the people of Okinawa has been rising 10.7 percent a year; the existing per capita income of around $300 provides a higher standard of living than that to be found in eight prefectures of the Japanese homeland. Other factors besides those concerned with economic improvement, however, must be taken into account. Final political authority is vested in a high commissioner appointed in Washington. An Executive Order of December,

1965, however, authorized the Ryukan Legislature to choose its own chief executive for a three-year term. The development of self-government thus approximates that achieved in the early North American colonies under the Hanoverian monarchy of England.

Perhaps of even more importance is the presence of some 50,000 military personnel with around 35,000 dependents cooped up on an island of 544 square miles that is already crowded with a teeming population of mixed Japanese, Chinese, and Polynesian ethnic strains. A very high level of social discipline would be required from the occupying forces to make their presence acceptable under colonial conditions of this character. Unfortunately, fair treatment and economic advancement are offset by the flaws in the American cultural pattern that foster expressions of race discrimination. A socially inferior status, beyond that imposed by differences in educational and economic opportunities, is granted all non-Caucasians through practices of unofficial segregation within the American military family itself. A *New York Times* correspondent described Old Koza, an entertainment quarter of Okinawa's second largest city, as a dreary example of Negro segregation with concomitant outbursts of race violence.[8] This reflects a pattern common to United States military installations in Korea and Japan, and the Army may not be blamed for conforming to conditions that result in part from policies of many state governments and the attitudes of some powerful political figures in Congress. However, this inherent incapacity to become socially integrated with the indigenous population sets sharp limits to the utility and duration of profitable American occupation. Okinawa's weakness as a keystone of United States security in the Pacific basin does not arise from immediately foreseeable subversion but rather from our failure to recognize that certain of our social policies are incompatible with long-term strategic needs. It would appear more prudent to concentrate strength on areas of proved loyalty, such as Guam, and then try to spread our influence over wider territories by accepting as fellow Americans the peoples who inhabit our far-flung military frontiers. Shortsighted reliance on continued military use of the lands of ethnic groups that we have no intention of admitting into our Union opens too many doors to resourceful adversaries.

American Samoa, 2,300 miles southwest of Honolulu, is an exception to the declared policies of the United States, specifically in reference to adherence to the United Nations declaration on independence for colonial peoples. It may be assumed, therefore, that strategic reasons exist for the continued occupation that may not be disclosed to the American public or the outside world for security reasons. No serious scandal arises from the continued tutelage of this pleasant community by diligent and well-intentioned administrators. However, the regional organization of Polynesian peoples, which is essential to Pacific development, is retarded by the political division of Samoa into colonial and independent regions.

Since 1951, when Samoa lost its status as a nonfloating command of the United States Navy, a limping administrative structure has been maintained by the Department of the Interior. Governors appointed by Washington came and went in rapid succession until 1956 when Presidential wisdom intervened to select a locally born resident as Governor. The constitutional standing of the territory is that of an insular possession of the United States—whatever that may mean—and the status of the indigenous inhabitants is that of "nationals" of the United States.

A bicameral legislature, the Samoan *Fono,* was created under naval administration and was reorganized in 1952 to allow elections under conditions of universal suffrage. The original upper house, the House of *Alii,* was composed wholly of hereditary chiefs and dominated the nonnoble lower Assembly. Under the reorganization plan, the House of *Alii* has become a straightforward Council of Paramount Chiefs with responsibility for advising the Governor on matters of Samoan ceremony and custom. The reorganized *Fono,* however, remains a strictly advisory body with no budgetary or lawmaking powers of its own.

The Samoan social organization is an anthropologist's paradise and is not readily adaptable to North American institutions. Basically, it is a society of autonomous villages comprised of related family groupings. The head of each extended family, the *matai,* exercises patriarchal authority, backed by a deep Samoan regard for rank. Each village has a council or village *fono* composed of the *matai.* Universal suffrage and equal representation fit uneasily into a social order of this character. Management of their own affairs in conjunction with the independent state of West Samoa would appear a practical alternative to continuance of an alien administration, however anthropologically well-informed and benevolent in intention.

Economic conditions among the 20,000 Samoans fail to reflect any considerable success for United States administration. In a basically agrarian society, with only 10 percent engaged as wage earners, food production is insufficient to meet consumption. Continually rising costs of imported foodstuffs have reduced real income over the course of the last few years. Ambitious young men tend to seek employment outside of American Samoa, partly on account of the lack of any institution for higher learning or advanced technical training. The privilege of migrating to Hawaii or the continental United States is one of the most concrete accorded Samoan "nationals"; however, it is harmful to the future of the Pacific homeland to be drained of its more energetic talents.

Although no malfeasance can be charged against the United States administration of Samoa, the introverted parochialism that fails to recognize one section of the whole island of Samoa as part of a regional Pacific entity handicaps the formation of a combined Western policy for the Pacific realm. To the State Department, and perhaps even the Pentagon, New Zealand is presumably one of the United States' most dependable partners in policy planning and implementation for the Pacific basin. The Department of the Interior, however, is engrossed in housekeeping activities and lacks the capacity to integrate its Samoan responsibilities with that of its friendly neighbors, thus condemning the region to piecemeal planning and development. Formulation of an overriding national policy embracing all aspects of United States territorial possessions in the Pacific realm is an overdue obligation of the President and Congress.

9 • THE UNITED STATES
ALLIANCE NETWORK

A tangled web—lacking overt intention to deceive—might constitute a charitable description of United States relationships entered into in piecemeal fashion throughout Asia and the Pacific since 1946. Historically, each and every one of them may be justified in view of the situation at the time, but the end result, achieved without any guiding schemata, is at least perplexing. An enumeration of reciprocal obligations may illustrate the situation. A special relationship is accorded the Philippine Republic based on defense arrangements that guarantee the republic's territorial integrity in return for United States use of military installations; particular economic ties also arise from agreements that terminated the political connection with the United States; in addition, both countries may be committed to limited common action in Southeast Asia through their mutual membership in SEATO. However, in the matter of the Philippines association in a regional confederation—the proposed Maphilindo or some other—the United States has had little to say and has allowed the initiative to pass into British and Indonesian hands. Presumably, if the Philippines enters into a regional pact, it will either sever its special relationship with the United States or commit this country to obligations that cover much more extensive areas. In plain fact, through a lack of any consensus on the future organization of the peninsular and insular regions of the Pacific and Indian oceans, the special relationship between the United States and the Philippines has dwindled to a tenuous connection based on transient convenience. The relationship remains merely dormant, however; it is still cradled in mutual goodwill and could be vigorously revived should a plan for Pacific security and development be evolved along lines attractive to both nations.

Some aspects of this special relationship between the two countries demonstrate the failure of the United States to formulate its objectives on a long-range basis. Present commercial and financial relations stem from a tidying up of the obligations of our former suzerainty. During the period of American rule, the Philippine economy was interlocked with ours, particularly through specially favored sugar imports and tariff-free trade. With political independence came a painful—at least in Filipino eyes—unraveling of these mutual economic ties. This was effected by the Bell Act of 1946, later emended in 1955, an arrangement that was dictated more by parochial United States interests than by any far-seeing conception of Pacific development. Through niggling bargaining and poor timing on the rates of tariff increases, the United States emphasized an apparent willingness to rid itself of past responsibilities for the economic growth of the Philippines and failed to substitute any mutually agreeable plan for future progress.

This economic separation has been pressed concurrently with a close military association that raises a suspicion of neocolonial use of Philippine territory. Generous financial assistance might have eased the situation if long-range objectives had been worked out in common. Unfortunately, the immediate postwar period was marked by a degree of corruption in Philippine politics that was matched by short-sighted and irresponsible United States actions. We poured about $2 billion into the country as compensation for war damages without taking proper safeguards to see that it would be used to promote economic growth. In consequence, the goodwill that should have resulted from a linkage of the economies of the two nations failed to materialize. Instead, a considerable section of the rural and laboring population detected an odor of corruption and sensed that they were being used and then abandoned. The bickering over terms of further war damage compensation irritated the sensitivity of the Philippine government and people to the point where it led to the cancellation of a proposed visit of President Macapagal to the United States in 1962. When the United States belatedly passed an acceptable Philippine war damage bill in August, 1962, President Kennedy hailed it "as a reaffirmation of the United States' intention to honor a long-standing moral commitment to the Filipino people." [1] However, the time lag in fulfilling this intention may have soured the results.

The military association has transcended arrangements

for the mutual defense of the republic's territory. The Military Bases Agreement of 1947 gave the United States a ninety-nine-year lease over twenty-three bases of varying size, with considerable powers of jurisdiction over the occupants. (The right to use seventeen of these base areas was surrendered in 1965.) Because two of these areas, Iloilo and the Clark Air Force Base, are important factors in the United States exercise of military power in the Pacific and Indian oceans, the Republic of the Philippines is inevitably involved in the total structure of United States policies in the Far East. But there is no reason to believe that this would prove unacceptable to the Filipino people if mutually acceptable terms of partnership and ultimate objectives were negotiated. Membership in SEATO as the principal link to United States policies is not enough. A political alliance sufficiently strong to compensate the Philippine Republic for the risks it runs as a springboard of United States power in the Pacific must be framed in more explicit terms to cover a wider field than that of anticommunism.

As an Asian power responsible for its policies before its peers, the Philippines must demonstrate its de facto independence and treat the United States only as a partner and ally united with it on common ends. It is the United States failure to formulate objectives that reach beyond anticommunism that brings into question the stability of the special relationship. Sooner or later, internal politics within the Philippines will make an issue of American military bases that involve that country in United States Asian policies. In the absence of clear United States commitments to advance Philippine interests within a mutually agreed-upon framework of policy for the Pacific realm as a whole, it will not be easy for Filipino supporters of partnership with the United States to resist such attacks.

Taiwan exemplifies another special relationship where arresting communist gains has overshadowed plans for a lasting association. In terms of diplomatic technicalities, the United States and her allies conquered Taiwan in the war with Japan. Its disposal to the Kuomintang forces, by way of a general order of August 15, 1945, issued under the authority of General Douglas MacArthur, does not confer diplomatic recognition. Though the Japanese Peace Treaty of 1952 stripped Japan of her fifty-year possession of Formosa and the Pescadores, the islands were not awarded to any other sovereign power. Consequently, postwar Taiwan exists in a diplomatic limbo where its de facto situation of "being loaned to a friend" receives practical recognition. United States relations with Taiwan are conducted in comparative isolation from its European associates in the Pacific, Britain and France, who have hesitated to join in the confusion. Another complicating factor is the presence of 9 million more or less indigenous Taiwanians, who remain distinct from the 2 million members of the Kuomintang who migrated there.[2] A procedure popularized by the United Nations would be to conduct a fairly supervised plebiscite of all the inhabitants to determine what form of government they desire. This step has not yet been considered practical by the present rulers or their United States protectors. It may be assumed that overriding defense considerations related to communist expansion inhibit any change in the status quo. On the other hand, since China ceded the island to Japan in 1895, Communist China possesses only sentimental claims based on contiguity and ethnic association. The problem, of course, is part of the larger issue of the nature of the uneasy truce in an undeclared war between the United States and Communist China. Because of the special relationship between Taiwan and the United States—which has cost the United States more than $4 billion in military and economic aid since 1951— Nationalist Chinese forces from Taiwan might be employed to assist anticommunist regimes struggling for survival in South Vietnam and elsewhere. However, a Taiwan report that United States specialists were training Nationalist troops for this purpose evoked prompt denial from the State Department in May, 1964.[3]

The keystone of the edifice of United States power in the Pacific realm is the special relationship with Japan that has nullified the opposition to the United States that arose there following its defeat in war. Japan provides an ideal bridge between Western technologies and the predominantly agrarian societies of Asia. This link depends, however, upon an agreement on common ends. Because this issue is still unresolved in both economic and political terms, the integration of Japan into a Western association is tenuous. Though its military collapse wrote finis to Japanese expansion through a "Greater East Asia Co-Prosperity Sphere" and similar dreams of power dominance, the withdrawal of the Japanese economic potential from Asian development occasioned a vacuum that could not be wholly filled by energetic shuttlings of the Seventh Fleet. The West must decide to what degree it will use Japanese industry and skills in the task of transforming the economic base of the Pacific region and, perhaps consequent to such a decision, what measure of reliance it will accord Japan as a military ally.

Present security arrangements with Japan originated in a treaty, signed in conjunction with the San Francisco Peace Treaty, that granted the United States an exclusive right to station forces in Japan that could be "utilized to contribute to the maintenance of international peace and security in the Far East" (Article 1). This was a conqueror's *dictat* that avoided even the *quid pro quo* of United States commitment to defense of Japanese territory. Revision of this one-sided pact became a major issue in domestic Japanese politics during succeeding years, though an American military "presence" in Japan appeared to be acceptable to the bulk of the electorate. In 1960, negotiations culminated in a new Treaty of Mutual Co-operation and Security. This treaty contained a preamble that designated as a common aim of both countries, "the maintenance of international peace and security in the Far East." To further this end, the United States retained its military bases within Japan but promised mutual consultation when the security of Japan or the Far East was threatened (Article 4). An equivocal clause in Article 1 that both parties would refrain "from the threat or use of force against any other state," would appear, superficially at least, to place a bit in the teeth of American operations in the Far East. According to modern diplomatic usage, however, no country ever threatens or attacks another, in its own reckoning, but merely reacts to unwarranted aggression. The 1960 treaty probably served the purpose of a sop to Japanese dignity without bringing to a troublesome head questions on the use of American bases as staging areas for general Asian wars or the delicate matter of future obligations of Japan to provide military assistance to United States causes. In this connection, it may be noted that the United States has spent almost $1.5 billion in helping Japan to rearm since 1950. A growing weakness of the Japanese military arrangement lies in its strictly bilateral character, which leaves the ANZAC nations, Britain, France, and the more remote SEATO associates outside the defense perimeter. From this point of view, United States policy coincides with Western interests only in the unacceptable character of sole protagonist.

The technological and industrial predominance of Japan in the Pacific area is an inescapable fact that affects any stable balance of power—military, economic, or political. From the Western viewpoint, its inescapability is matched by its awkwardness: the expansion of Japanese trade involves commercial rivalry with the narrow national interests of individual Western nations.

Before World War II, Japan's exports to Asia accounted for 60 percent of her total exports. With regard to the import of essential raw materials, from 1934 to 1936 China supplied 34 percent of Japan's imports of iron ore, 68 percent of her coal, and 71 percent of her soya beans. Today, though the United States supplies approximately equivalent percentages of Japan's needs, the Japanese claim that the price of coal imported from China is 54 percent below that brought from the United States, and iron ore is 32 percent lower. At present, the three main areas of Japan's trade—Asia, North America, and the rest of the world— are almost equal in scope; hopes of expansion in Europe or Latin America, however, depend on the uncertain goodwill of the European Common Market or on United States interests.

Logically, Japan should be considered in the forefront of nations equipped to meet the demands of technologically underdeveloped peoples, in terms of its capacity to produce economically both an infrastructure of construction machinery and electrical equipment and low-price consumer goods. Her opportunities for fulfillment along these lines, however, depend more on the political policies of the powerful Western nations than on the competitive conditions of an open market. An increasingly independent Japan is being accosted by the economic charms of China and Russia, who are trying to weaken its dependence on the United States. A Sino-Japanese trade pact of 1962 provided some opportunity to raise the 1 percent of Japan's total trade with the Chinese mainland to a level more consistent with the historical figure. Soviet wooing of the Japanese economy can and does dangle the bait of a future share in the industrialization of Siberia. Though the West could use Japan's industrial potential for the technological development of Asia, it is a wasting asset from the political point of view, one that may even revert to the opposition unless it is provided a swift and fair outlet through joint action.[4]

Perhaps the most dangerous illusion harbored by the United States concerning relations with Japan is that they may be preserved as an exclusive relationship. It is only within the framework of a Pacific union paralleling the Atlantic union that Japan can be assured of proper standing as a Western associate. Though superficially minor, a needless irritant in relations between Japan and the United States is maintained through discriminatory immigration quotas imposed by the United States Congress. In return for residence rights in Japan of over 100,000 American military and civilian personnel and their dependents, the United States grants Japan an annual immigration quota figure of 185, which may be compared with Finland's 566 and Yugoslavia's 942.[5]

A special relationship with Australia was thrust upon the United States by the contingencies of war, with little preparation or preliminary diplomatic understanding. Historians may unravel the puzzle as to why the United States resisted Australian pleas for mutual consultations and arrangements before Pearl Harbor. In any case, the retreat from the Philippines exposed the United States need for a continental base from which to stage an effective offensive into the Far Pacific. It may be presumed that missile warfare has not materially diminished this requirement in the face of possible future contingencies. Wartime comradeship did not altogether eradicate the mutual reluctance of Australia and the United States to cement intimate relations. To the United States, jealous of its exclusive control over Japan's postwar organization and increasingly absorbed in the anti-communist struggle in Southeast Asia, Australia tended to assume a supernumerary character. An apparent downgrading of the significance of the Australian economy as an instrumentality for uplifting standards throughout the Pacific area, coupled with impatience of limitations imposed on the use of Australian territory for American military purposes, marked negotiations prior to the signing of the Japanese peace treaty.

On the Australian side, the difficulty of adjusting from traditional reliance on Britain to the new reality of United States predominance played its part. Basically, Australia's objective is, and has been for a considerable period, the achievement of a regional pact covering the whole South Pacific area and involving continental and peninsular Asia only insofar as its constituent nations threatened to intrude into the oceanic realm. The scope of such a pact would include economic development as well as defense requirements and would provide Australia with responsibilities and privileges that recognized her capacities and geographical situation. No true meeting of minds has taken place between United States and Australian statesmen on this central issue. Asian wars of subversion have captured United States attention to the exclusion of interest in the establishment of a consolidated base for Western influence throughout the whole Pacific realm.

In consequence, the special relationship between Australia and the United States is based on a series of compromises that are not fully satisfactory to either party. The key ANZUS Treaty of 1951, involving Australia, New Zealand, and the United States in defense arrangements against the possibility of Japanese resurgence and aggression from Communist China and more vaguely from other quarters was primarily a military posture. The mutuality of obligations is greater, however, than appears on the surface, for the pact imposes on Australia a duty to coordinate its military establishment with that of the United States, so as to serve as an effective joint base when needed. A casual denigration of British power in the Pacific, implied by the exclusion of the United Kingdom from the treaty, has now come home to roost. Parallel military arrangements between Britain, Australia, and New Zealand under the designation ANZAM, have involved the ANZAC countries in the Indonesian confrontation of Malaysia. Without taking any initiative of its own and deprived of an opportunity to coordinate events with its own policy lines, the United States has been nudged into the position of a military backer of a British-ANZAC guarantee of Malaysian integrity.

An unresolved aspect of United States–Australian relations centers around the traditional Australian islands policy. Originally conceived in terms of defense planning, this policy may be outmoded, in part, by developments in air and missile warfare. However, feelings in the antipodean countries regarding secure control of contiguous island chains parallels, to some extent, United States sensitivity in respect to the Caribbean area. Britain, through long Commonwealth association, recognizes Australia's legitimate interest, particularly with regard to the future of Fiji and the New Hebrides. In 1955 and again in 1958, the United Kingdom transferred control over the Cocos-Keeling Islands and Christmas Island, respectively, from the colony of Singapore to the Commonwealth of Australia. These tiny island groups could conceivably possess strategic value to Australia as watchdogs for her near northern approaches.

The major instrument of United States diplomatic hegemony in the Pacific and Indian oceans is the Southeast Asia Collective Defense Treaty (SEATO), operative since 1955. It may be claimed that the obligations undertaken by the United States under the terms of this treaty are no greater than, or of a different nature from, those that her general policy line would have indicated as acceptable had no treaty existed. The reliance placed on the treaty by American statesmen is, accordingly, based on its value in committing other nations to United States policies in the region. In its origins, SEATO fulfilled Australian ambitions to bind together the antipodean nations, the United States, and as many Asian states as possible in a general pact to ensure the peace of the region. It was not until the collapse of France in Indochina that the United States showed interest in the project. Preliminary negotiations were clouded by a dispute with the United Kingdom, which wanted a pact embracing India and the major states of Asia, with, of course, the exception of Communist China.[6] In 1954, the United States considered the crisis in Laos of paramount importance and was unwilling to stretch its commitments. Accordingly, the grand design of a comprehensive Western–Asian alliance was discarded in favor of a limited and ambiguous arrangement. In its final form, the treaty resembled a diplomatic net—loopholes connected by tenuous threads—rather than a firm bond.

Article 8 defined the "treaty area" as the general area of Southeast Asia, including also the entire territories of the Asian parties to the treaty, and the general area of the Southwest Pacific, but not including the Pacific area north of latitude 21° 30′. The latter provision was inserted on the demand of the United States in order to exclude Taiwan and Hong Kong from the terms of the treaty. For varied reasons, Asian states in general distrusted the final form of the treaty, and only Pakistan, Thailand, and the Philippines linked themselves with the Western members—the United States, the United Kingdom, France, Australia, and New Zealand. A peculiar diplomatic device, however, in the form of a protocol to the treaty, virtually conscripted South Vietnam, Cambodia, and Laos—though they had not accepted membership—as areas "designated" under treaty protection at any time their respective governments consented to such intervention.

The nature of the defense provisions contained in Articles 2 and 4 were unusually ambiguous. Article 2 binds the parties to achieve the objectives of the treaty "by means of continuous and effective self-help and mutual aid [which] will maintain and develop their individual and collective capacity to resist armed attack and to prevent and counter subversive activities directed from without against their territorial integrity and political stability." This "counter subversion" clause is difficult to interpret in practical terms; it apparently opens the door to intervention by the parties in the domestic affairs of member and designated states, perhaps at the behest of minorities in temporary control of the governmental apparatus.

Article 4 approaches more closely to the specificity of NATO arrangements in declaring that "each Party recognizes that aggression by means of armed attack in the Treaty Area against any of the Parties or against any State or territory which the Parties, by unanimous agreement may hereafter designate, would endanger its own peace and safety, and agrees that it will in that event act to meet the common danger. . . ." At this point, the article departs from a firm commitment that would parallel the NATO pledge and ends lamely with the phrase, "in accordance with its constitutional processes." If this qualification means anything at all, it implies that each government will decide according to the political exigencies of the moment whether it chooses to be bound by its treaty obligations in terms of action.

A further limitation on obligations under the treaty is contained in the following "Understanding of the United States of America," embodied in the treaty as a concluding clause: "The United States of America in executing the present Treaty does so with the understanding that its recognition of the effect of aggression and armed attack and its agreement with reference thereto in Article 4 paragraph 1 apply only to Communist aggression but affirms that in the event of other aggression or armed attack it will consult under the provisions of Article 4 paragraph 2." It was, and still remains, the intention of the United States to employ the SEATO treaty principally as an instrument in the struggle to contain communism in Asia and the Pacific. For this reason, SEATO membership has come to be regarded by Asian states as an open enlistment in a United States anticommunist crusade that involves the likelihood of concentrated hostility on the part of mainland China. Even as friendly a state as Malaya on attaining independence declined to accept this degree of partnership with the West.

A structural form was provided for operation of the SEATO treaty with a Secretariat stationed at Bangkok. The Council of Ministers which meets annually is the supreme directive body, though representatives of the parties hold frequent *ad hoc* meetings. A permanent Military Planning Office, served by expert committees, is part of the staff organization. This represents a minor form of military coordination when compared to the Supreme Commander's office of NATO. Economic and cultural cooperation is designated as a treaty objective in Article 3, and civilian staffs undertake projects along these lines. In almost every case, however, they duplicate work that would fall normally under the auspices of the Colombo Plan or other existing agencies.

It may not be denied that SEATO has proved a convenience to United States diplomacy in meeting the specific crises that have arisen in Southeast Asia. The cost of this convenience, however, comes high. An original opportunity to link the bulk of Asian and Pacific states with major Western nations in a protective alliance for the maintenance of peace and order throughout the Pacific and Indian ocean regions has been jettisoned and perhaps is now irretrievably lost. In its place, a United States-dominated bloc, with lagging partners, has revived Asian fears of Western hegemony. Further, the evasion of responsibility by the concurring powers inhibits a realistic formulation of policies that could stimulate true joint endeavors by the major Western powers and their Asian and Pacific associates. France, by declining to join in the chorus of approval of South Vietnam policies at the May, 1964, SEATO meeting, perhaps served the West well. Policy aims for which individual participants are not prepared to venture their men or money are dangerous hypocrisies that conceal whatever true area of agreement exists.

In general, the grid of diplomatic and military arrangements through which United States power makes itself felt in the Pacific bears an unhappy resemblance to a spider's web. All lines of communication run to the center, where the dynamic strength of the Seventh Fleet lurks; lateral communication among the supporting allies is inadequate for the operation of a working partnership. The formulation of a conjoint Western policy in which each nation would participate to the extent of its interests at stake continues to be inhibited by a fragmentation of relations. Though Western concepts for the development of the Pacific realm appear more likely to achieve the social advancement of the people than communist ideology, the voice of the West is silenced until its component nations can agree on a declaration of objectives. No single nation, however powerful, can speak for the Western complex in the absence of joint debate, resolution, and commitment to implementation. A congress of the Pacific should not be conceived along propaganda lines; the preliminary task of reconciling interests and allotting functions is a major diplomatic undertaking. A growing sense of limitations on the capacity of the United States to serve as the sole arbiter of the Pacific region should speed this essential confrontation.

10 • THE PROSPECTS OF REGIONALISM

The preceding arguments have indicated that Western influence in the Pacific realm must be anchored in a base of regional organization. Yet regions do not present themselves as ready-made geographical or cultural entities; their existence owes more to political art than to accidents of contiguity. Two factors may be said to predominate in the creation of a regional organization: one is a compelling motivation for closer association inside the area, and the other is pressure by outside parties intent on gaining spheres of influence within a definite geographical region. The concept of regional organization as applied to the Pacific realm would rely on the first principle to bring about closer ties between the nations of the Maphilindo complex and almost wholly, at least during an initial stage, on metropolitan influence for effective grouping of the peoples of the island chains.

The opportunities open to Western nations to pursue policies of regional organization in order to achieve greater solidarity between the peoples of the West and the Orient should be evaluated in the light of an existing framework of ideological assumptions and practical political and military control over specific areas. United States policy, at least as expressed through the Department of State and through Congress, tends to treat Asia as a single diplomatic sphere in which United States interests may be promoted through the balancing of contending interests without full identification with, or commitment to, any specific grouping. This, of course, is a classic Western attitude, inherited from the colonial period and somewhat unfairly designated as a "divide and rule" policy. One weakness of this concept, from the point of view of the preservation of Western interests, is that it puts North American and European powers in the role of intruders into the affairs of indigenous peoples who are organized as independent nations. The proclamation of an obligation—superior to that of national interest—to preserve world order and uphold the charter of the United Nations may be countered by a demand that any such action be implemented through the collective procedures of the United Nations organs. Unless the United States is prepared to acknowledge that she is a Pacific power, by right of her responsibilities and possessions in a specific, though limited, section of the region, her intervention in the power struggle of the Far East is likely to be regarded as piratical by uncommitted nations.

In the flux of contemporary Asian politics, several potential regional groupings appear possible. The Sino-Communist bloc, composed of mainland China, North Korea, and North Vietnam, is already consolidated in its unchanging hostility to the United States. Other peninsular states of Southeast Asia—Thailand, South Vietnam, Laos, and Cambodia—have found no common bond of political association; their individual dependence on, or rejection of, United States support contributes to the international turmoil of the area. India, Burma, and Ceylon—with Pakistan temporarily sulking in its tents—remain aloof from Western alignments under a shadowy canopy known as the Colombo powers. The peoples of Malay origin—Malaysia, Indonesia, and the Philippines—are still in critical dispute over the political orientation of a Maphilindo association. Should Indonesia predominate, their association with the West would be sharply curtailed, whereas under favorable circumstances of Malaysian or Philippine direction, an alliance—political and economic, if not military—with Britain and the United States might be anticipated. However, a truly Western-oriented region within the Pacific realm must seek its base in the antipodean nations in association with island possessions of the Western powers. Though sufficient political, economic, and military power remains in the hands of the West to consolidate territorial possessions into an operative region that could be defended against both external aggression and internal subversion, the will to implement this objective has not yet manifested itself on the higher level of national policies. On lower administrative levels, however, interconnections have been achieved that indicate the general design of a Pacific region that the Western powers could create and sustain. A survey of present conditions may suggest possibilities that are within the power of governments to implement, when and if they can formulate comprehensive objectives for a Pacific realm.

Such an examination could be commenced by studying the full text of the Multilateral Pacific Charter subscribed to by SEATO signatories on September 8, 1954. As an expression of pious goodwill, it is binding on the contracting parties, however unaware they may have shown themselves to be of the significance of their commitment.

> Delegates. . . . Desiring to establish a firm basis for common action to maintain peace and security in Southeast Asia and the Southwest Pacific.
>
> Convinced that common action to this end, in order to be worthy and effective, must be inspired by the highest principles of justice and liberty.
>
> *Do hereby proclaim*
>
> First, in accordance with the United Nations Charter they uphold the principle of equal rights and self-determination of peoples, and they will earnestly strive by every peaceful means to promote self-government and to secure the independence of all countries whose peoples desire it and are able to undertake its responsibilities.
>
> Second, they are each prepared to continue taking effective practical measures to insure conditions favorable to the orderly achievement of the foregoing purposes in accordance with their constitutional processes.
>
> Third, they will continue to cooperate in the economic, social and cultural fields in order to promote higher living standards, economic progress and social well-being in this region.
>
> Fourth, as declared in the Southeast Asia Collective Defense Treaty, they are determined to prevent or counter by appropriate means any attempt in the treaty area to subvert their freedom or destroy their sovereignty or territorial integrity.[1]

If the provisions of the first, second, and third clauses of the Pacific charter had been applied by the United States, Britain, and Australia to joint management of their own possessions in the area, foundations for a functional Pacific region would already exist. Neglect of treaty obligations by governments, however, is as often due to ignorance of the implications of their statesmen's rhetoric as it is to bad faith. In the specific case of the Pacific charter, the intent to cooperate remains a binding declaration despite the lack of substantial implementation.

Before 1954, an instrumentality for the furtherance of administrative and economic cooperation in the Southwest Pacific had been launched under the name of the South Pacific Commission. This body, which had been initiated by Australia and New Zealand in 1944 to advance their islands' policies, was made operative through the participation of Britain, France, the Netherlands, and the United States in 1948. The principle of a joint endeavor by the metropolitan powers to improve social, economic, and administrative conditions among their 4 million wards scattered over thirteen square miles of the Pacific Ocean was unexceptionable. In the opening words of the agreement, the participating governments stated their desire "to encourage and strengthen international cooperation in promoting the economic and social welfare and advancement of the non-self-governing territories in the South Pacific region administered by them." [2] Why this high resolve has brought forth such minor accomplishments might be due to faulty organization of the administrative apparatus, insuperable obstacles in the way of attainment of objectives, or plain double talk on the part of the national policy makers concerned. In this writer's opinion, the last factor is overwhelmingly responsible for the laggard pace. In support of this view, it may be noted that the annual budget allotted for the work of the commission by all the participating nations is normally less than $1 million, a sum barely adequate for staff expenses. Nevertheless, this gallant skeleton, awaiting the flesh of political realism, has mapped out feasible plans for applying technological knowledge and skills to problems concerning the livelihood of South Seas peoples. In conjunction with the almost equally meager resources of United Nations agencies, it has outlined attacks on health problems and arranged for the transmission of skills to indigenous peoples so that they can participate in directing their own advancement. A recital of the commission's achievements, despite its ludicrously inadequate resources, would bring as much honor to its technical and administrative staff as it should bring censure to the political budgeteers.

Of course, the financial starvation of the South Pacific Commission is no mere matter of penny-pinching treasuries. It is a decision of high political policy that has been deliberately maintained. Old jealousies between erstwhile colonial powers are by no means dead; in fact, they have been invested with new life under the name of "strategic considerations." Before implementing their plans along lines indicated by the South Pacific Commission, the metropolitan powers concerned must first resolve their own intramural difficulties. In the first place, what will be the political base for administrative coordination throughout the area? The military and diplomatic interests of Australia, France, and the United States are far from identical, and Britain possesses considerable bargaining advantages through the extent of her holdings, if not the intensity of her concern. A possible tripod of Australia, Guam, and

Hawaii as contending loci for the dissemination of technical skills is further complicated by understandable French objections to monolithic Anglo-Saxon predominance in the region.

An even more serious issue is the true objective of each of the participating powers toward the future political status of the indigenous peoples, in view of the strategic tensions in the region. A saving clause in Article 13 of the agreement founding the commission states that "nothing in this Agreement shall be construed to conflict with the existing or future constitutional relations between any participating Government and its territories or in any way to affect the constitutional authority and responsibility of the territorial administrations." Clearly a major question at issue has been conveniently shelved. It would be armchair presumption to claim that solutions for these difficulties in accordance with national security considerations of the countries concerned are plainly indicated. What appears regrettable in terms of the advancement of Pacific peoples and the preservation of Western influence is the absence of discussion that would define the limits of the problem and weigh the penalties for failure to achieve a pragmatic resolution. In part, the rhetoric of treaties and agreements has overlaid the true nature of the responsibilities of the Western powers in the Pacific realm with a paralyzing veneer of diplomatic hypocrisy.

In its structural form, the commission sketches an elegant device for the future coordination of political and administrative control throughout the eighteen non-self-governing territories encompassed. As a nonsovereign condominium, the political center of the commission rests in a council of twelve commissioners, two from each participating nation, with voting rights confined to the senior commissioners of the member states. "The Commission shall be a consultative and advisory body to the participating Governments in matters affecting the economic and social development of the non-self-governing territories within the scope of the Commission and the welfare and advancement of their peoples" [Article 4]. Decisions are made on a majority basis except where financial contributions from the participating governments are concerned, and then unanimity is mandatory. Organs of the commission are the Research Council and the Secretariat. The larger question of social and political union is approached through the institution of the South Pacific Conference, a body that is auxiliary to the commission and serves "to associate with the work of the Commission representatives of the local inhabitants of, and of official and unofficial institutions directly concerned with, the territories within the scope of the Commission . . ." [Article 9, paragraph 27]. Delegates to this conference are appointed for each designated territory according to its own internal political rules with the proviso that "delegates shall be selected in such a manner as to ensure the greatest possible measure of representation of the local inhabitants of the territory" [Article 9, paragraph 35]. The conference meets approximately every three years for periods of less than a month—the fifth meeting was held in American Samoa in 1962; its functions are advisory with no budgetary or legislative powers delegated to it from the metropolitan sovereigns.

The apportionment of the South Pacific Commission's expenses indicates the degrees of commitment by participating nations: Australia bears the highest proportion, 30 percent; Britain and the Netherlands contribute 15 percent each; and the United States and France trail with contributions of 12.5 percent apiece. As prolegomena to effective social union, the administrative and consultative forms outlined by the South Pacific Commission appear to be ingeniously suited to the cultural environment. In the absence of nationalist feelings, party politics, or racial tensions among the indigenous inhabitants, solidarity may be advanced through a common attack on problems of welfare and economic growth by combining the technological skills that are at present monopolized by Western residents with the cooperative enterprise of the local community. Unfortunately, a divisive nationalism among the metropolitan powers themselves paralyzes the use of any means of achieving union that would not serve the national interest. In less than two decades of existence, however, the South Pacific Commission has demonstrated the feasibility of economic, technological, and social regionalism as a means for advancing the Pacific island peoples. Political implementation now rests on the shoulders of the metropolitan nations concerned. There are growing indications that the timing and manner of their decision will determine the issue of whether Western influence will be an integral factor in the future of the Pacific realm.

A wider framework for regional cooperation that concentrates wholly within the economic field is to be found in the Colombo Plan, which has been operating since 1951. Though it may be questioned whether the Colombo Plan is a truly regional apparatus, in view of its extension over the greater part of Southeast and South Asia, the adaptation of the system to specific political regions appears practicable. As described in the 1962 report of the plan's Consultative Committee:

it is a system under which the member countries help one another through the exchange of ideas and experience as well as through the provision of many forms of capital and technical aid. . . . One of the hopeful circumstances in the economic scene is the existence of a vast fund of accumulated knowledge in the advanced countries and in the more advanced parts of the developing countries. This fund is so great that many years of technical progress would be possible for the countries of the region even if no further scientific discoveries were made. The task is to spread this knowledge and spread the best techniques throughout the economy.[3]

From its beginnings as an enterprise of British Commonwealth countries, the plan has broadened to include twenty-two countries, sixteen within the region and six outside nations—Australia, Britain, Canada, Japan, New Zealand, and the United States. In its essence, the Colombo Plan is a clearing house for development projects and technical assistance. Agreements are made between cooperating governments on a bilateral basis; the United States, for example, distributed assistance amounting to $1.6 billion among thirteen participating countries during 1962.[4] Economic growth through comprehensive national planning is generally accepted among Asian Colombo Plan countries, and capital-aid projects have been financed to the tune of $6.3 billion during the first decade of operation. The heart of the scheme, however, lies in technical assistance. By extending help so that the countries of the region may be able to help themselves, technical assistance has proved a relatively inexpensive form of cooperation. Further pooling of national resources of trained skills has blurred an original distinction between outside donor nations and receiving members; India, Pakistan, Burma, Ceylon, Malaysia, Indonesia, the Philippines, and Thailand now rank as donors in respect to a sharing of training facilities.

A considerable advance in evaluating manpower resources at the technical level was achieved by a survey, known as the 1961 Mills Report, authorized by the Council for Technical Cooperation and made possible through a grant from the Ford Foundation. The main theme of the Mills Report was a clearly defined and rational approach to the problem of training within the region in order to overcome the failure of government technical departments, their educational counterparts, and industry in general throughout the region to coordinate their efforts. A gap in communication between professional engineers and craftsmen, together with an acute shortage of competent instructors in technical subjects, had previously slowed economic development processes.

In its structural form, the Colombo Plan is a nonpolitical and functional approach to international organization for economic development. Its guiding body, the Consultative Committee, composed of representatives from all participating countries, meets annually in various regional capitals for a brief session. It serves primarily as a discussion club for an exchange of views between senior officials and ministers of appropriate departments of the member states. In the communique of the 1962 report, a single sentence sufficed to summarize its activities: "the Consultative Committee reviewed economic developments in the region during the past year and the progress of the Colombo Plan, and an assessment was made of some of the tasks ahead of the countries of the region." Between meetings of the Consultative Committee, the Council for Technical Cooperation, composed of member states' ambassadors stationed within Ceylon, meets several times a year at Colombo to oversee the functioning of the one full-time organ, the Bureau of Technical Cooperation. A skeleton organization of this character inhibits the introduction of political questions and encourages the coordination of social and economic development below the level of rhetorical nationalism. Though too wide in its scope to rank as a true regional organization, there is nothing in the machinery of the Colombo Plan to hinder its application to more narrowly political regions, according to the desires of participating groups. In fact, jealousies and fears that might be stimulated by the formation of political regions may be assuaged through the framework of area meetings and the interchange of information established under the plan. Some of the elasticity of the Commonwealth concept has remained with the plan; reinforced by creation of effective political groupings within its area of operation, it might contribute considerably to the solidarity of mankind.

A further development is the institution of an Asian Development Bank, which was proposed by the United Nations in 1964 and implemented by United States participation since 1966. When signing the Congressional bill authorizing American commitment of funds, President Lyndon B. Johnson described the bank as "an economic Magna Carta for the diverse lands of Asia." [5] This statement may verge on hyperbole, for the total capitalization of the bank is only $1 billion, whereas previous United States assistance to Asian countries since World War II has amounted to $20 billion. The American contribution is an annual sum of $20 million over a five-year period, with an additional $100 million on call for a special fund primarily for economic development in Southeast Asia. Nineteen Asian countries will contribute 65 percent of the bank's capital, and the rest will come from the United States, Britain, Canada, West Germany, Belgium, Denmark, Italy, and the Netherlands. France has not chosen to participate. The headquarters of the bank is located in Manila, and its president and a predominant proportion of its staff are Asian. Thus the Asian Development Bank is at least a gesture toward Western collaboration in the economic self-development of Asian peoples.

Peripheral to the Pacific realm lie the inhospitable wastes of Antarctica, a region that impinges on the world of politics mainly in terms of vague and unforeseeable contingencies. The shadow of Antarctica, however, serves to stimulate closer political association among Western powers throughout the whole Pacific area. In the particular case of the United States, territorial claims recognizable by international law that might provide a footing in this blank region are noticeably meager. Accordingly, the exercise of American influence depends heavily on understandings and agreements with New Zealand, Australia, and Britain, who have established claims to vast holdings of unproductive real estate that retain some validity in international law and diplomatic practice. It is reasonable to ask why bother about uninhabitable lands possessing immediate value only as scientific laboratories, and the only answer is that nobody knows what unexpected advances in science and technology may eventuate to thrust the South Pole into prominence in world strategy, communications, or even productivity. Sound statesmanship requires that so unpredictable an area be at least placed under political wraps until more certain knowledge of its potentialities is forth-coming.

Soviet intrusion into Antarctica after World War II stimulated the United States to develop a policy for this region; before that time, its concern may be fairly described as tangential.[6] On the diplomatic initiative of the United States, all interested states negotiated and ratified a treaty in 1959 that dedicated Antarctica to peaceful uses and prohibited military fortification and installations and any military measures in the area by any of the contracting parties. However, the controversial issue of the validity of claims to sovereign rights over poorly defined areas by European nations, Australia, New Zealand, Argentina, and Chile remained unsettled. A saving clause in the treaty reserved all such claims with a proviso that no new claim or enlargement of a previous claim be asserted during the thirty-year life of the treaty (Article XIV). Though this treaty safeguarded American global interests by preventing the utilization of Antarctica as a hostile military base, it left the United States in a weak position in terms of territorial rights for the purpose of scientific and geographic research. Despite a lack of claimed territory, an accommodation with New Zealand in the form of a memorandum that allowed for a virtual exchange of resource and logistic facilities sufficed for the establishment and maintenance of scientific centers. In the long run, United States interests in Antarctica—should that frozen region ever develop significance in world economy or power strategy—depend for the most part on close association with Australia and New Zealand. To this extent, Antarctica has become a factor in the promotion of a Pacific realm where the influence of Western nations can be implemented through the undertaking of mutual responsibilities extending beyond the scope of military alliances.

It would seem cavalier to conclude a discussion of the prospects of regionalism in the Pacific realm without assessing contributions from the United Nations. If the concept of regionalism is to be interpreted strictly, however, only one United Nations-sponsored organization, the Economic Commission for Asia and the Far East (ECAFE), may be viewed as promoting regional solidarity. As in the case of the Colombo Plan, the region envisaged embraces all Asia, extending well beyond the Pacific realm. Also, ECAFE implemented its wider scope in political terms by including the Soviet Union and China among its members. As a result, however, joint planning and cooperative action became impracticable, at least for the foreseeable future. Founded in 1947, ECAFE's objectives were to facilitate concerted action for the economic development of Asia, to strengthen economic relations within the region, and to promote relations with outside countries. As a center of information, fact-gathering, and objective evaluation of economic developments, ECAFE has rendered invaluable services to the region. It was never intended that it should become an aid-distributing agency for South and Southeast Asia. As its membership is composed of communist, Western, and nonaligned Asian nations, it is precluded from any consensual formulation of economic objectives that involve political action.

11 • SOME SPECULATIONS

Politics, though not the most productive of mankind's activities, remains the arbiter of social organization. Economic, ethnic, and cultural ties are, for the most part, building stones that can be erected in multiform designs according to the will of the political architect. This study has concerned itself with social materials and existing administrative patterns available for arrangement under Western hands into the political structure of a Pacific realm. Whether or not such a realm should be created raises a question of high policy subject to a consensus of Western statesmanship. A survey of possibilities should determine the basic constituents of policy making, recognizing that decisions by power holders are affected by many factors extraneous to ideal blueprints. Speculation has value, however, if only to clarify the kind of choices open on the level of pragmatic statesmanship.

Some assumptions appearing throughout this book may be summarized in support of a Pacific realm as a desirable objective of United States policy. In the first place, in the sphere of strategic balance, the posture of the United States in the Far East suffers from the lack of a social and economic base that would justify as well as support the exercise of military power. The stigma of sea-borne intruder vitiates some of the legitimate claims of the United States to participate in the affairs of the Orient. In the second place, effective United States action in the Pacific region should be related to the institutional framework resulting from the colonial epoch. An important incentive to development will be willingness and capacity to undertake co-operative enterprises with the inheritors of that period—indigenous power groups as well as European economic, political, and administrative structures. Further, pressures for regional solutions to problems of economic and cultural stagnation will increase rapidly, determining by their strength and direction ultimate political patterns. Conflict regarding the establishment and preservation of cultural spheres of influence among the island peoples of the Pacific is likely to be intensified through a Chinese apparatus of communist expansion.

In light of the foregoing assumptions, the question of unified Western policy making and implementation in the Pacific realm merits reevaluation. One bold approach would involve a recasting of the North Atlantic alliance to cover an Eastern as well as a Western sphere of influence. This solution, suggested by a former President of the West German Bundestag, Dr. Eugen Gerstenmaier, includes the formation of two interlocking ellipses, with Washington, armed with United States nuclear power, as the center of both.[1] Paris, according to Dr. Gerstenmaier, could serve as the bastion of the Western zone and Tokyo that of the Eastern zone. SEATO, and presumably ANZUS, would merge into this global expansion of NATO. The plan has the merit of subordinating the divisive jealousies inherited from the colonial epoch to realities of Western survival in a changed world. Recognition of Japan as a key partner with the West in the Pacific and Indian ocean regions might ease part of the burden at present carried by the United States. The Netherlands, Belgium, Italy, and other nations of the European community, besides France, could be restored to participation in Pacific and Asian affairs. The harmful exclusiveness of the "colonial club" would be mitigated as a factor of the Western presence in the Pacific and Indian oceans.

Yet the obstacles in the path of this ambitious project are formidable. In the first place, cooperation with major Asian nations on the basis of open alliance might meet increasing resistance in the face of a unified Western presence. This form of partnership, however, is of questionable significance under existing circumstances. Among the Asian nations subscribing to SEATO, only the Philippines may be regarded as an important addition to Western strength. Retention of military installations in Malaysia and the Philippines by Britain and the United States respectively provides a temporary rather than a permanent base for the exercise of effective power. The involvement of independent nations in warlike situations without their consent is militarily as well as diplomatically unsound, subjecting vital staging areas to the risk of immobilization from political causes at times of severe crisis. From Hawaii to Guam and the strategic trust territories, the United States controls staging areas for military power that may be employed independently of any other nation. Okinawa, however, remains essential to the exercise of American force throughout the Orient; this fact raises significant questions about the degree of close association with Japan that may prove desirable to underwrite the United States position as arbiter of Pacific and Asian affairs.

Among the Western nations, France might prove reluctant to correlate her Asian and Pacific policies with those of the English-speaking nations. But the choice of promoting or disregarding increased Western solidarity in relations with Asian and Pacific peoples rests, in the final analysis, with the United States. Since she possesses most of the actual force available for application in the region and bears the lion's share of the consequent burdens, this country must determine the extent of her willingness to share responsibilities with Western allies. Concessions to joint deliberation might prove as severe as those incurred in the operation of NATO within the Atlantic zone. On the other hand, it is questionable whether the United States possesses sufficient power to counter, through its unaided efforts, the communist and nationalist challenges to any Western presence in the Pacific realm.

Great Britain, acting in association with Australia and New Zealand, is in a good position to play the honest broker both between the United States and the European nations and to a lesser extent between a single Western complex and such Asian nations as India and Malaysia. With its military and economic strength in the Far East seriously diminished, the long-term interests of Britain point to the acceptance of partnership in responsibility.

It is time to heed the warning conveyed by Nehru at the 1956 Bandung Conference:

> I should like to say that we sit with the great countries of the world as brothers, be it in Europe or America. . . . we want to be friends with them to cooperate with them. But we shall only cooperate in the future as equals; there is no friendship when nations are not equal, when one has to obey the other and when one dominates the other. That is why we raise our voice against domination and colonialism from which many of us have suffered so long and that is why we have to be very careful to see that any other form of domination does not come in our way. . . . Australia and New Zealand are almost in our region. They certainly do not belong to Europe, much less to America. They are next to us and I should like indeed Australia and New Zealand to come nearer to Asia. There they are. I would welcome them because I do not want what we say or do to be based on racial prejudices. We have had enough of this racialism elsewhere.[2]

A tragedy for all mankind would ensue from the withdrawal of the Western nations from the Far East, or even their relegation to the status of external trading entities. Technology has created a new social environment that demands greater, not less, solidarity among individuals and societies if unimaginable catastrophes are to be avoided. Now, even more than in the days of Adam Smith, commerce—in the sense of a mutual interchange of different experiences of living, as well as material goods—has become the proper business of mankind. Governments should be constituted to achieve this end within and without their territories, with diplomacy, war, and rule serving as instruments to promote conditions favorable to the solidarity of mankind.

notes •

INTRODUCTION: A NOTE ON
THE PACIFIC REALM

1. This discussion of regional nomenclature is based on an article by the Geographer of the State Department, G. Etzel Pearcy, "Geographic Regions of Asia: South and East," a reprint from *The Department of State Bulletin* (February 1, 1960), rev., Department of State Publication No. 7262 (Washington, D.C., 1961).

2. The geographer Richard Hartshorne describes the concept of a "realm" as follows: "A major world segment, or realm, may also be recognized on the basis of coherent unity of its various parts, however diverse in character, have closer political relations with each other, whether those of co-operation or of conflict, than they have with areas outside its limits . . ." Richard Hartshorne, "What Is Political Geography?" in P. E. Jones and C. F. James, eds., *American Geography, Inventory and Prospects* (Syracuse, N.Y.: Syracuse University Press, 1954), p. 187. The term "Pacific

realm" is employed as a chapter heading in Harold J. Wiens, *Pacific Island Bastions of the United States* (Princeton, N.J.: Van Nostrand, 1962).

CHAPTER 1: THE WEST AND
THE PACIFIC REALM

1. Harold J. Wiens, *Pacific Island Bastions of the United States* (Princeton, N.J.: Van Nostrand, 1962).
2. The latest development at the time of writing is The Association of Southeast Asian Nations which has been constituted by Indonesia, Malaysia, Singapore, the Philippines, and Thailand as an economic and cultural group. Formation at Bangkok reported in *The New York Times,* August 10, 1967.
3. Estimates concerning British trade with the East quoted from Saul Rose, *Britain and South-East Asia* (Baltimore: Johns Hopkins University Press, 1962), p. 64.
4. *Economic Survey of Asia and the Far East, 1962* (New York: United Nations, 1963), p. 56.
5. *Economic Survey of Asia and the Far East, 1964* (New York: United Nations, 1965), p. 215.
6. *Economic Bulletin for Asia and the Far East,* XIII, 3 (December, 1961), 69.

CHAPTER 2: THE CONSEQUENCES OF
WESTERN DOMINION

1. Sir Alfred Lyall (Indian Civil Service, 1856–1887), quoted in Sir George Dunbar, *India and the Passing of Empire* (New York: Philosophical Library, 1952), p. 45.

CHAPTER 3: THE CHARACTER OF
BRITISH INTERESTS

1. Richard Goold-Adams, "Report of the Political Sub-Committee," in *The Future of the Commonwealth: a British View* (London: Her Majesty's Stationery Office, 1963).
2. Figures quoted from J. H. B. Tew, "The Economic Relationships of the Commonwealth," in *The Future of the Commonwealth.*
3. Tom Soper, "Report of the Economic Sub-Committee," in *The Future of the Commonwealth.*

4. *Report of the Commission of Enquiry into the Natural Resources and Population Trends of the Colony of Fiji, 1959* (Burns Report) (London: Crown Agents for the Colonies, 1960).

5. A/C. 4/L. 849. U.N. General Assembly. Twenty-first session. Fourth Committee Agenda item 69. December 8, 1966. New York.

6. "In 1964, China sent a record $320 million worth of food, clothing, and other products to Hong Kong. This represented a 23 percent increase over the 1963 total. Since China's imports from Hong Kong amounted to only $10 million, its net earnings in freely convertible foreign exchange were $310 million. "Invisible" earnings in the form of remittances from overseas Chinese to relatives on the mainland and from Chinese Communist banking and commercial interests in the colony are estimated to bring China at least $200 million more. Hong Kong is therefore a source of more than 40 percent of the foreign exchange earned by China annually." *The New York Times,* January 18, 1965.

CHAPTER 4:
THE MALAYSIAN FEDERATION

1. *Malaysia; Agreement etc.* Cmnd. 2094. (London: Her Majesty's Stationery Office, July, 1963).

2. Statement by British Prime Minister Harold Wilson, reported in *The New York Times,* January 8, 1965.

3. Figures quoted from Willard Hanna, "The Singapore Base," in *Malaysia, Federation in Prospect,* Part VII. American Universities Field Staff Report Service, Southeast Asia Series, Vol. X, No. 11, September, 1963.

4. Cmnd. 1794 (London: Her Majesty's Stationery Office, 1962).

5. T. E. Smith, *The Background to Malaysia* (Oxford: Oxford University Press, 1963), p. 3.

6. *Ibid.,* pp. 16–18. Also Lo Kuan Yew, *The Battle for Merger* (Singapore: Government Printing Office, 1962); and *Memorandum of the Barisan Sosiates Party of Singapore.* Mimeographed document (Singapore: March 11, 1963).

7. *The New York Times,* August 6, 1963.

8. *The New York Times,* June 13, 1963.
9. *The New York Times,* May 31, 1967.

CHAPTER 5:
THE POLICIES OF INDONESIA

1. Speech by President Sukarno on Independence Day (August 17), 1963, quoted from Bruce Grant, *Indonesia* (Melbourne: Melbourne University Press, 1964), p. 46.
2. *Ibid.,* p. 17.
3. Benjamin Higgins, *Indonesia: The Crisis of the Millstones* (Princeton, N.J.: Van Nostrand, 1963), p. 65.
4. *The New York Times,* December 20, 1963.
5. *Economic Survey of Asia and the Far East, 1962* (New York: United Nations, 1963), p. 168.
6. Lecture by Sukarno to the students of Hasnudden University, quoted from Paul Sigmund, *The Ideologies of the Developing Nations* (New York: Praeger, 1963), p. 59.
7. An analysis of the Eight-Year Plan by an expert who served as financial consultant in Indonesian affairs may be found in Benjamin Higgins, *op. cit.,* Ch. 6.
8. Figures quoted from Grant, *op. cit.,* p. 84.
9. *The New York Times,* April 20, 1963.
10. Grant, *op. cit.,* p. 38.
11. A study of the linguistic problems of Indonesian nationhood may be found in Ben Anderson, "The Language of Indonesian Politics," *Indonesia* (Journal of the Cornell Modern Indonesia Project), Vol. 1 (April, 1966).

CHAPTER 6:
FRANCE IN THE PACIFIC

1. Jacques Stern, *The French Colonies* (New York: Didier, 1944), p. 13.
2. Alain Huetz de Lemps, *L'Océanie française* (Paris: Presses Universitaires de France, 1954), p. 86.
3. *The New York Times,* March 8, 1964.
4. Gerald Coppenrath, "Evolution politique de la Polynésie

Française depuis la Première Guerre Mondiale," *Journal de la Société des Océanistes*, Vol. XV, No. 15 (December, 1959).

CHAPTER 7: THE PLACE OF THE ANTIPODEAN NATIONS: AUSTRALIA AND NEW ZEALAND

1. Report of a statement by the then Undersecretary of State Averell Harriman at Brisbane, *The New York Times*, June 4, 1963.
2. *The New York Times*, June 4, 1963.
3. *Cambridge History of the British Empire*, Vol. VII, Part One, *Australia* (New York: Macmillan, 1933), p. 502.
4. *The New York Times*, January 19, 1964.
5. *Christian Science Monitor*, March 12, 1963.
6. Acceptance of a World Bank report as a basis for planning the economic development of Papua–New Guinea has committed the Australian government to massive spending in agriculture and other primary industries. The Australian Minister for Territories announced preliminary planning for a scheme similar to the American Peace Corps and for financial development. *The New York Times*, May 25, 1965.
7. Two of the leading Australian advocates of a Melanesian federation are J. R. Kerr, former Secretary of the South Pacific Commission, and J. Andrews, Lecturer in Geography at the University of Sydney. See J. R. Kerr, "The Political Future," and J. Andrews, "New Guinea and Australia's Defence and Foreign Policy," in Australian Institute of Political Science, *New Guinea and Australia* (Sydney: Angus and Robertson, 1958).
8. *The New York Times*, October 13, 1964.

CHAPTER 8: THE TERRITORIAL STAKE OF THE UNITED STATES

1. Introduction by Marshal of the Royal Air Force, Sir John Slessor to *Collective Defence in South East Asia* (London: Royal Institute of International Affairs, 1956), p. xiii.
2. *Report of the United Nations Visiting Mission to the Trust*

Territory of the Pacific Islands, 1964, Trusteeship Council Documents (New York: United Nations, 1964), p. 60.

3. The appointment of Richard F. Taitano, a native of Guam, as Director of the Office of Territories and subsequently (in 1964) as Deputy High Commissioner of the Trust Territory was indicative of enlightened executive interest. Also the selection of M. Wilfred Goding, an Alaskan, as High Commissioner of the Trust Territory vitalized administration in the field, insofar as sparse funds would permit, during his 1961–1966 term of office.

4. Department of State, *Trust Territory of the Pacific Islands, 1963,* p. 16. Department of State Publication No. 7676 (Washington, D.C., 1964).

5. *Report of the United Nations Visiting Mission to the Trust Territory of the Pacific Islands, 1964,* p. 53.

6. *Report of the United Nations Visiting Mission to the Trust Territory of the Pacific Islands, 1964,* p. 159.

7. *The New York Times,* January 14, 1964.

8. *The New York Times,* March 29, 1964.

CHAPTER 9: THE UNITED STATES ALLIANCE NETWORK

1. *Department of State Bulletin,* Vol. XLVII, No. 1208 (August 20, 1962).

2. This estimate is taken from Allen S. Whiting and Robert A. Scalapino, "The United States and Taiwan," in Willard L. Thorp, ed., *The United States and the Far East,* 2nd ed. (Englewood Cliffs, N.J.: Prentice-Hall, 1962).

3. *The New York Times,* May 14, 1964.

4. For an analysis of United States–Japan trade and economic relations, see Robert A. Scalapino, "The United States and Japan," in Thorp, *op. cit.*

5. *The New York Times,* June 27, 1963.

6. See Charles O. Lerche, "The United States, Great Britain and SEATO: A Case Study in the *Fait Accompli,*" *Journal of Politics* (August, 1956).

CHAPTER 10: THE PROSPECTS
OF REGIONALISM

1. Multilateral Pacific Charter, September 8, 1954.
2. Ruth C. Lawson, *International Regional Organization* (New York: Praeger, 1962), p. 255.
3. *The Colombo Plan: Eleventh Annual Report of the Consultative Committee*, Cmnd. 1928 (London: Her Majesty's Stationery Office, 1963), pp. 27, 31.
4. For a breakdown of United States contributions (in pounds sterling) between capital assistance and technical cooperation to individual countries between 1950 and 1962, see L. P. Singh, *The Colombo Plan, Some Political Aspects*, Appendices B and C. Canberra Department of International Relations (Canberra: The Australian National University, 1963).
5. *The New York Times*, March 17, 1966.
6. A comprehensive review of the discoveries in Antarctica and the resulting international claims may be found in C. Hartley Grattan, *The Southwest Pacific since 1900* (Ann Arbor: University of Michigan Press, 1963).

CHAPTER 11:
SOME SPECULATIONS

1. *The New York Times*, October 24, 1964.
2. Quoted from George McTurnan Kahin, *The Asian-African Conference* (Ithaca, N.Y.: Cornell University Press, 1956), pp. 73, 75.

selected source material •

The selected source material listed for each chapter refers to the content of the text. Comprehensive bibliographies for background information may be found in the books listed, and no attempt has been made to duplicate them for particular areas in this volume.

CHAPTER I: THE WEST AND THE PACIFIC REALM

Books

Two major works that provide essential background material are the following:

Grattan, C. Hartley, *The Southwest Pacific since 1900.* Ann Arbor, University of Michigan Press, 1963.

Kahin, George McTurnan, *Governments and Politics of Southeast Asia,* 2nd ed. Ithaca, N.Y., Cornell University Press, 1964.

The books listed below deal with specific issues:

Battistini, Lawrence H., *The Rise of American Influence in Asia and the Pacific*. Ann Arbor, University of Michigan Press, 1960.

Clubb, Oliver E., Jr., *The United States and the Sino-Soviet Bloc in Southeast Asia*. Washington, D.C., Brookings Institution, 1962.

Edwardes, Michael, *Asia in the Balance*. Baltimore, Penguin Books, 1962.

Grattan, C. Hartley, *The United States and the Southwest Pacific*. Cambridge, Mass., Harvard University Press, 1961.

Panikkar, K., *Asia and Western Dominance*. London, Allen and Unwin, 1953.

Rose, Saul, *Britain and South-East Asia*. Baltimore, Johns Hopkins University Press, 1962.

Staley, Eugene, *The Future of Underdeveloped Countries*. New York, Praeger, 1961.

Thorp, Willard L., ed., *The United States and the Far East*, 2nd ed. Englewood Cliffs, N.J., Prentice-Hall, 1962.

Weins, Harold J., *Pacific Island Bastions of the United States*. Princeton, N.J., Van Nostrand, 1962.

Reports

Economic Bulletin for Asia and the Far East, 1961, 1962, 1963, et seq. New York, United Nations.

Economic Policies Toward Less Developed Countries. Joint Economic Committee, Congress of the United States, 87th Congress, 1st Session. Washington, Government Printing Office, 1961.

Economic Survey of Asia and the Far East, 1962 et seq. New York, United Nations, 1963.

Articles

Morison, S. E., "American Strategy in the Pacific Ocean." *Oregon Historical Quarterly*, Vol. 62 (March, 1961).

CHAPTER 2: THE CONSEQUENCES OF WESTERN DOMINION

Books

Adam, Thomas R., *Modern Colonialism: Institutions and Policies.* Garden City, N.Y., Doubleday, 1955.

Bourgeau, J., *La France du Pacifique.* Paris, Collection Terres Lointaines, 1950.

Easton, Stewart C., *The Twilight of European Colonialism.* New York, Holt, Rinehart and Winston, 1960.

Emerson, Rupert, *From Empire to Nation.* Cambridge, Mass., Harvard University Press, 1960.

Furnivall, J., *Colonial Policy and Practice.* London, Cambridge University Press, 1948.

Huetz de Lemps, Alain, *L'Océanie française.* Paris, Presses Universitaires de France, 1954.

Koebner, R., and H. D. Schmidt, *Imperialism.* New York, Cambridge University Press, 1964.

Simnett, W. E., *The British Colonial Empire.* New York, Norton, 1942.

Stern, Jacques, *The French Colonies.* New York, Didier, 1944.

Strausz-Hupé, Robert, and Harry W. Hazard, eds., *The Idea of Colonialism.* New York, Praeger, 1958.

CHAPTER 3: THE CHARACTER OF BRITISH INTERESTS

Books

Burns, Sir Alan, *Fiji.* London, Crown Library. Her Majesty's Stationery Office, 1963.

———, *The Future of the Commonwealth: a British View.* London, Her Majesty's Stationery Office, 1963.

Morrell, W. P., *Britain in the Pacific Islands.* New York, Oxford University Press, 1960.

Rose, Saul, *Britain and South-East Asia.* Baltimore, Johns Hopkins University Press, 1962.

Simnett, W. E., *The British Colonial Empire*. New York, Norton, 1942.

Stanner, W. E. H., *The South Seas in Transition*. Sydney, Australasian Publishing Company, 1953.

West, Francis, *Political Advancement in the South Pacific*. Melbourne, Oxford University Press, 1961.

Reports

British Islands in the Southern Hemisphere. Cmnd. 8230, London, Her Majesty's Stationery Office, 1951.

Colonial Reports: British Solomons, 1960; New Hebrides, 1960; Fiji, 1960. London, Her Majesty's Stationery Office.

The Colonial Territories, 1961–1962 (and previous years). Cmnd. 1751, London, Her Majesty's Stationery Office.

Non-Self-Governing Territories, Summaries of Information Transmitted to the Secretary-General for 1961, "Pacific Territories." New York, United Nations, 1963.

Progress of the Non-Self-Governing Territories under the Charter, Vol. 2, *Economic Conditions,* 1960, and Vol. 5, *Territorial Surveys,* 1960. New York, United Nations.

Special Study on Social Advancement in Non-Self-Governing Territories. New York, United Nations, 1962.

Technical Co-operation: A Progress Report by the Department of Technical Co-operation. Cmnd. 1698, London, Her Majesty's Stationery Office, 1963.

Articles

Allen, C. H., "Local Government in the British Solomon Islands." *Journal of African Administration* (July, 1960).

West, F. J., "Problems of Political Advancement in Fiji." *Journal of African Administration* (April, 1961).

CHAPTER 4:
THE MALAYSIAN FEDERATION

Books

Dobby, E. H. G., *Southeast Asia*. London, University of London Press, 1958.

Farmer, J. N., "Malaysia," in George McTurnan Kahin, ed., *Governments and Politics of Southeast Asia*, 2nd ed. Ithaca, N.Y., Cornell University Press, 1964. This chapter contains a comprehensive bibliography concerning Malaya and the formation of the federation.

Jones, S. W., *Public Administration in Malaya*. London, Oxford University Press, 1953.

Smith, T. E., *The Background to Malaysia*. Chatham House Memorandum. London, Oxford University Press, 1963.

Winstedt, Sir Richard O., *Malaya and its History*, 5th ed. London, Hutchinson's University Library, 1958.

Reports

American Universities Field Staff Reports Service, Southeast Asia Series, Vol. X, No. 11 (Brunei, Malaya, North Borneo, Sarawak, Singapore), 1962–1963.

Malaysia: Agreement Concluded between the United Kingdom of Great Britain, etc., the Federation of Malaya, North Borneo, Sarawak and Singapore, 1961. Cmnd. 2094, London, Her Majesty's Stationery Office.

Malaysia: Report of the Inter-Governmental Committee (Lansdowne Report), 1962. Cmnd. 1954, London, Her Majesty's Stationery Office, 1963.

Report of the Commission of Enquiry: North Borneo and Sarawak. Cmnd. 1794, London, Her Majesty's Stationery Office, 1962.

Articles

Armstrong, Hamilton Fish, "The Troubled Birth of Malaysia." *Foreign Affairs* (July, 1963).

CHAPTER 5:
THE POLICIES OF INDONESIA

Series Books

The publications of the Modern Indonesia Project at Cornell

University provide the most comprehensive review of the area for American readers. Among the works in this series are the following:

Feith, Herbert, *The Decline of Constitutional Democracy in Indonesia*. Ithaca, N.Y., Cornell University Press, 1962.

Kahin, George McTurnan, "Indonesia," in Kahin, ed., *Major Governments of Asia*, 2nd ed. Ithaca, N.Y., Cornell University Press, 1963.

———, *Nationalism and Revolution in Indonesia*. Ithaca, N.Y., Cornell University Press, 1952.

McVey, Ruth T., and H. Benda, eds., *The Communist Uprisings of 1926–1927 in Indonesia: Key Documents*. Cornell Modern Indonesia Project, Translation Series. Ithaca, N.Y., Cornell University Press, 1960.

Soedjatmoko, *Economic Development as a Cultural Problem*. Cornell Modern Indonesian Project, Translation Series. Ithaca, N.Y., Cornell University Press, 1958.

———, *An Approach to Indonesian History: Towards an Open Future*. Cornell Modern Indonesian Project, Translation Series. Ithaca, N.Y., Cornell University Press, 1960.

Taylor, A. M., *Indonesian Independence and the United Nations*. Ithaca, N.Y., Cornell University Press, 1960.

Books from General Sources

Brackman, Arnold C., *Indonesian Communism: A History*. New York, Praeger, 1963.

Furnivall, J., *Netherlands India: A Study in Plural Economy*. New York, Macmillan, 1944.

Grant, Bruce, *Indonesia*. Melbourne, Melbourne University Press, 1964.

Hanna, Willard A., *Bung Karno's Indonesia*. New York, American Universities Field Staff, Inc., 1960.

Higgins, Benjamin J., *Indonesia: The Crisis of the Millstones*. Princeton, N.J., Van Nostrand, 1963.

McVey, Ruth T., "Indonesian Communism and the Transition to Guided Democracy," in A. Doak Barnett, ed., *Communist Strategies in Asia*. New York, Praeger, 1953.

————, ed., *Indonesia.* New York, Taplinger, 1963.
Pauker, Guy J., "The Role of the Military in Indonesia," in J. J. Johnson, ed., *The Military in the Underdeveloped Areas.* Princeton, N.J., Princeton University Press, 1962.

Articles

Hindley, Donald, "President Sukarno and the Communists: The Politics of Domestication." *American Political Science Review,* Vol. LVI, No. 4 (December, 1962).
Mackie, J. A. C., "Indonesia: A Background to Confrontation." *The World Today* (April, 1964).
Pauker, Guy J., "Indonesia in 1963: The Year of Wasted Opportunities." *Asian Survey,* Vol. IV, No. 2 (February, 1964).

CHAPTER 6:
FRANCE IN THE PACIFIC

Books

Belshaw, Cyril S., *Changing Melanesia: Social Economics of Culture Contact.* Melbourne, Oxford University Press, 1954.
Bourgeau, J., *La France du Pacifique,* Paris, Collection Terres Lointaine, 1950.
Deschamps, H., and Jean Guiart, *Tahiti, Nouvelle-Caledonia, Nouvelles-Hebrides.* Paris, Editions Berger-Levrault, 1957.
Grattan, C. Hartley, *The Southwest Pacific since 1900.* Ann Arbor, University of Michigan Press, 1963.
Huetz de Lemps, Alain, *L'Océanie française.* Paris, Presses Universitaires de France, 1954.
Stern, Jacques, *The French Colonies.* New York, Didier, 1944.
West, Francis, *Political Advancement in the South Pacific.* Melbourne, Oxford University Press, 1961.

Reports

Non-Self-Governing Territories, Summaries of Information for 1961, Vol. 5, *Territorial Surveys,* New Hebrides section. New York, United Nations, 1960.
Progress of the Non-Self-Governing Territories under the Charter,

Vol. 5, *Territorial Surveys*, New Hebrides section. New York, United Nations, 1960.

Articles

Coppenrath, Gerald, "Evolution politique de la Polynesie française depuis la Première Guerre Mondiale." *Journal de la Société des Océanistes*, Vol. XV, No. 15 (December, 1959).

Cumberland, Kenneth B., "The Future of Polynesia." *The Journal of the Polynesian Society* (December, 1962).

"French Polynesia." *South Pacific Bulletin* (January, 1963).

West, Francis, "Local Government in French Polynesia and American Samoa." *Journal of Local Administration Overseas*, Vol. II (July, 1963).

Note: Detailed bibliographies of France in the Pacific may be found in the following periodicals:

Bulletin bibliographique du Ministère de la France d'Outre-mer. Paris.

Bulletin de la Société des Etudes océaniennes. Papeete.

Journal de la Société des Océanistes. Paris, Musée de l'Homme.

CHAPTER 7: THE PLACE OF THE
ANTIPODEAN NATIONS:
AUSTRALIA AND NEW ZEALAND

Books

Australian Institute of Political Science, *New Guinea and Australia*. Sydney, Angus and Robertson, 1958.

Beaglehole, Ernest, *Social Change in the South Pacific: Rarotonga and Aitutaki*. New York, Macmillan, 1957.

Belshaw, Cyril S., *Changing Melanesia: Social Economics of Culture Contact*. Melbourne, Oxford University Press, 1954.

The Cambridge History of the British Empire, Vol. VII, Part One, *Australia*. New York, Macmillan, 1933.

Essai, Brian, *Papua and New Guinea*. Melbourne, Oxford University Press, 1961.

Gordon, B. K., *New Zealand becomes a Pacific Power.* Chicago, University of Chicago Press, 1960.

Grattan, C. Hartley, *The Southwest Pacific since 1900.* Ann Arbor, University of Michigan Press, 1963.

Mair, L. P., *Australia in New Guinea.* London, 1948.

Morrell, W. P., *Britain in the Pacific Islands.* New York, Oxford University Press, 1960.

Pacific Islands Year Book, 8th ed. Sydney, 1959 *et seq.*

Stanner, W. E. H., *The South Seas in Transition.* Sydney, Australasian Publishing Company, 1953.

West, Francis, *Political Advancement in the South Pacific.* Melbourne, Oxford University Press, 1961.

Reports

Non-Self-Governing Territories, Summaries of Information Transmitted to the Secretary-General for 1961, "Pacific Territories." New York, United Nations, 1963.

Official Records of the Trusteeship Council, Thirtieth Session, Plenary, May 29 to June 26, 1963. New York, United Nations, 1963.

Progress of the Non-Self-Governing Territories under the Charter, Vol. 5, *Territorial Surveys.* New York, United Nations, 1960.

Special Study on Social Advancement in Non-Self-Governing Territories, 1957–1959. New York, United Nations, 1962.

United Nations Visiting Mission, *Report on New Guinea, 1962,* in *Official Records of the Trusteeship Council,* Twenty-Ninth Session, Supplement No. 3. New York, United Nations, 1962.

Articles

Bell, Cora, "Australia and the American Alliance." *The World Today* (July, 1963).

Leifer, Michael, "Australian Trusteeship and New Guinea." *Pacific Affairs,* Vol. XXXVI, No. 3 (Fall, 1963).

Pacific Islands Monthly. Sydney. A news magazine published since 1930.

Tate, M., "Australian Monroe Doctrine." *Political Science Quarterly* (June, 1961).

CHAPTER 8: THE TERRITORIAL STAKE OF
THE UNITED STATES

Books

Coulter, J. W., *The Pacific Dependencies of the United States.*
New York, Macmillan, 1957.

Hobbs, W. H., *The Fortress Islands of the Pacific.* Ann Arbor,
University of Michigan Press, 1944.

Keesing, Felix M., *The South Seas in the Modern World.* New
York, John Day, 1941.

Pratt, J. W., *America's Colonial Experiment.* Englewood Cliffs,
N.J., Prentice-Hall, 1950.

Stevens, Russell L., *Guam, U.S.A.: Birth of a Territory.* Honolulu, Tongg Publishing Co., 1956.

Weins, Harold J., *Pacific Island Bastions of the United States,*
Princeton, N.J., Van Nostrand, 1962.

West, Francis, *Political Advancement in the South Pacific,* Chap.
IX, "American Samoa." Melbourne, Oxford University Press,
1961.

Reports

Center for Cultural and Technical Interchange between East and
West (East-West Center), hearings before the Committee on
Foreign Affairs, House of Representatives, Eighty-Seventh
Congress, December 13 and 14, 1961, and January 8, 1962.
Washington, D.C., Government Printing Office, 1962.

*The Governor of American Samoa to the Secretary of the Interior,
1961 Annual Report.* Washington, D.C., Government Printing
Office. See also reports for 1962, 1963, *et seq.*

*The Governor of Guam to the Secretary of the Interior, 1961
Annual Report.* Washington, D.C., Government Printing Office. See also reports for 1962, 1963, *et seq.*

Progress of the Non-Self-Governing Territories under the Charter,
Vol. 5, *Territorial Surveys,* Chap. VIII, "Pacific Territories."
New York, United Nations, 1960.

*Report of the United Nations Visiting Mission to the Trust Ter-
ritory of the Pacific Islands, 1961, in Official Records of the*

Trusteeship Council, Twenty-Seventh Session. New York, United Nations.

Trust Territory of the Pacific Islands, 1963, 16th annual report to the United Nations on the administration of the Trust Territory of the Pacific Islands. Department of State Publication No. 7676, Washington, D.C., 1964.

CHAPTER 9: THE UNITED STATES ALLIANCE NETWORK

Books

Black, Joseph E., and Kenneth W. Thompson, eds., *Foreign Policies in a World of Change.* New York, Harper, 1963. The following selections are pertinent: Saul Rose, "The Foreign Policy of Britain"; Y. Sito, "The Foreign Policy of Japan"; Robert A. Scalapino, "The Foreign Policy of the People's Republic of China"; Kenneth W. Thompson and Joseph E. Black, "The Foreign Policy of the United States of America."

Burks, Ardath W., *The Government of Japan,* 2nd ed., Chap. 11, "The Foreign Relations of Japan." New York, Crowell, 1964.

Grattan, C. Hartley, *The United States and the Southwest Pacific.* Cambridge, Mass., Harvard University Press, 1961.

Lerche, Charles O., *Foreign Policy of the American People.* Englewood Cliffs, N.J., Prentice-Hall, 1958.

Rose, Saul, *Britain in Southeast Asia.* Baltimore, Johns Hopkins University Press, 1962.

Rostow, W. W., *The United States in the World Arena.* New York, Harper, 1960.

Thorp, Willard L., *The United States and the Far East,* 2nd ed. Englewood Cliffs, N.J., Prentice-Hall, 1962.

Ward, Robert, E., and Roy C. Macrides, eds., *Modern Political Systems of Asia.* Englewood Cliffs, N.J., Prentice-Hall, 1963.

Articles

Bell, Cora, "Australia and the American Alliance." *The World Today* (July, 1963).

Johnsone, William C., "A New Look at American Policy in Southeast Asia." *Sais Review* (Spring, 1961).

Hilsman, Assistant Secretary of State, "The Challenge to Freedom in Asia." *The Department of State Bulletin* (July 8, 1963).

Thomas, M. Ladd, "A Critical Appraisal of SEATO." *Western Political Quarterly* (December, 1957).

CHAPTER 10: THE PROSPECTS
OF REGIONALISM

Books

Grattan, C. Hartley, *The Southwest Pacific since 1900,* Chapters XII–XV, "Antarctica." Ann Arbor, University of Michigan Press, 1963.

Lawson, Ruth C., *International Regional Organization.* New York, Praeger, 1962.

Manders, L. A., *Some Dependent Peoples.* New York, 1959.

Singh, L. P., *The Colombo Plan: Some Political Aspects.* Canberra, Australian National University, 1963.

Reports

The Colombo Plan, Eleventh Annual Report of the Consultative Committee. Cmnd. 1928, London, Her Majesty's Stationery Office, 1963.

Reports of the South Pacific Commission, 1961–1963 et seq. Tahiti, South Pacific Commission.

Technical Co-operation under the Colombo Plan, report for 1961–1962 of the Council for Technical Co-operation in South and Southeast Asia. London, Her Majesty's Stationery Office, 1962.

Articles

Andrews, J., "Defence and Foreign Policy," and J. R. Kerr, "The Political Future," in Australian Institute of Political Science, *New Guinea and Australia.* Sydney, Angus and Robertson, 1958.

Tate, M., "Australian Monroe Doctrine." *Political Science Quarterly* (June, 1961).

index •